Jennifer Faith takes you on an inspiring journey from abuse to freedom. I highly recommend her book, which will bring faith and hope to all who read it.

— Alan Garrett, author of *UNSilenced:*
Giving a Voice to Women Silenced by Ignorance
and pastor of Mountain of Worship, Manchester CT

The Dark Night of Faith is an amazing story that everyone living in an abusive situation should read and share with others. Jennifer's compelling story reveals her strengths and weaknesses and tells how God gave her the power to leave and survive. She recovers, with God lifting her in His grace and mercy, and gives all the glory to Him.

— Pamela East PhD,
author, educator, survivor of abuse, and
certified facilitator for Advocacy for Victims of Abuse
and Mending the Soul ministries

The Dark Night
of Faith

By

Jennifer Faith

Deep River
B O O K S

The Dark Night of Faith

© 2021 by Jennifer Faith

Published by Deep River Books
Sisters, OR
www.deepriverbooks.com

ISBN: 9781632695345
Library of Congress Control Number: 2021946200

Cover design by Robin Black, Inspirio Design
Printed in the USA

For my sister.

Thank you for always being there for your li'l sis. I would not have made it through this life without you.

ACKNOWLEDGMENTS

To the family members, friends, prayer partners, pastors, legal professionals, shelter volunteers, and counselors who supported me in my journey out of the darkness—I am alive today because of you. Thank you for being willing instruments in the hands of my loving Heavenly Father. I would also like to thank Andy Carmichael and Deep River Books for finding my story and giving me a chance to tell it. And a very big thank you to my editor, Kit Tosello. I will forever be grateful for the skill, care, grace, and respect with which you treated my story.

CONTENTS

FOREWORD

Since 1981, October has been recognized as National Domestic Violence Awareness Month. Domestic violence affects millions across our nation, both women and men, of every race, religion, culture, and status. As a pastor I feel I have an obligation, not just to my church family but also to our greater community, to join other voices that make known the presence and dangers of domestic abuse.

Each October we set aside one Sunday as Domestic Violence Awareness Sunday. During a worship service, we remind our people of our responsibility to stand against domestic violence and serve as agents of healing for both the abused and the abuser. We do this through prayer and lament, through the reading of Scriptures that speak of God's love and presence, and through the teaching of biblical passages that speak to abuse and our role as healers. Out of this desire to help bring healing to those who have been abused, our churched birthed Advocates for Victims of Abuse (AVA) and Mending the Soul Ministry. It was in this context that I first met Jennifer Faith. Jennifer had been asked by the leaders of our AVA ministry to lead a Sunday afternoon workshop during Domestic Violence Awareness Month. We also invited Jennifer to share her story during our Sunday morning services.

Jennifer's story touched a chord not only in my heart, but also in many others that Sunday morning. It's one thing to talk about domestic abuse and quite another to hear directly from someone who has suffered its tragic consequences. It raised questions in my mind. How many Jennifers were there in my congregation? How many of my neighbors or those in my community were living out Jennifer's story? The National Coalition Against Domestic Violence (NCADV) reports that "1 in 4 women and 1 in 7 men have been victims of severe physical violence (e.g. beating, burning, strangling) by an intimate partner in their life-time."[1] And of course, these statistics don't take into account other forms of abuse. In addition to physical abuse, the US Department of Justice recognizes an additional four: sexual, emotional, economic, and psycho-logical abuse.

In Jennifer's story, like so many others, spousal abuse reaches beyond the closed doors of the involved adults. It traumatically affects the well-being of the couple's children. In a *Psychology Today* article titled "Alarm-ing Effects of Children's Exposure to Domestic Violence," they write, "The Centers for Disease Control and Prevention have reported that in homes where violence between partners occurs, there is a 45% to 60% chance of co-occurring child abuse, a rate 15 times higher than the aver-age. Even when they are not physically attacked, children witness 68% to 80% of domestic assaults. These numbers are a sobering reminder of the toll a violent environment takes on kids."[2] Spousal abuse also draws in and can divide other family members, as each party makes their case and looks for the family support they need.

The effects of abuse also follow the abuser and the abused into the workplace. A 2001 report by the Centers for Disease Control and Pre-vention titled "The Costs of Intimate Partner Violence Against Women in the United States" states, "The annual cost of lost productivity due to domestic violence is estimated as $727.8 million, with over 7.9 million paid workdays lost each year."[3] And of course, abuse comes at a great personal financial cost, as the family unit addresses additional medical expenses, counseling and mediation fees, legal fees, and the potential costs connected to moving, separate housing, and ongoing support. Abuse has great economic costs.

The effects of abuse are great, but Jennifer Faith had the courage not only to persevere but to write about her experiences in the midst of her many dark days. But hers is not just a story of personal struggle. It is about her quest for and discovery of a sustaining faith which brought comfort and healing during times of questions and darkness. I believe her story will resonate with all readers and especially with those who have faced or currently face abuse. It speaks of days, even years, of being silent when protecting the marriage was the top priority. It speaks of secrets and isolation when she felt no one else could understand.

Her story is the story of many who have been physically abused, emotionally battered, constantly manipulated, and left feeling, "It must be my fault!" For Jennifer, as well as others like her, the result is a loss of self-esteem and self-respect. For many, these scars and feelings began in earlier years, when perhaps as a child they were abused or told they were worthless.

But are we worthless? Each of us have certain truths or lies we believe about ourselves. Jennifer references author Brennan Manning as he describes how our impostor self often battles with our true self, and the question becomes, "Who am I going to believe?" She says Manning's *Abba's Child* is must–read, and I couldn't agree more. As a young follower of Jesus, I wrestled with my personal identity and pondered questions like *Who am I?* and *What is true about me?* I was fortunate to hear Manning speak in Colorado, and one of his statements has stayed with me. He said, "There is nothing you can do that will cause God to love you more than he does today." The truth is that I am deeply loved by God. I am accepted by him as having great worth and value, no matter what others may say.

For the abused, like Jennifer, this becomes a powerful and liberating truth. As her story will illustrate, this truth has to be told and heard not just once but over and over again. These truths about our worth and value to God and others can redefine our life and give us the power to stand against the lies of the abuser and against the lies of Satan himself. In order for us to start believing what is true, there must be a community who will support us and remind us of these things. Like she says, we need a dolphin pod that we can swim with. We can't survive on our own. We can only begin to be truthful with ourselves when we are willing to be truthful with God and others.

For Jennifer, her faith in God and the support of those around her made her freedom possible. Jesus once said, "You shall know the truth and the truth will set you free." You may or may not be a person of faith, but I hope you will read Jennifer's story and, through it, find the courage you need to move forward into truth and new areas of freedom and healing in your life.

Senior Pastor Jack Snell
Puna Covenant Church

INTRODUCTION

When I began writing this book, I had a secret. Not just any old secret. My most highly guarded secret. One that I'd gone to great lengths for over two decades to protect. Doing so consumed my life. In fact, it was on the verge of killing me. Until . . .

He came.

Jesus. He reached out his tender, nail-scarred hands and said that if I held on to him, he would rescue me—but I couldn't hold on to my secret and him too. This was a terrifying choice. But something in his eyes made me sure . . . he would not ask me to let go of my plan unless he had a better one. So I opened my hands, let go, and grabbed on to him with everything in me.

This is the story of how Jesus traded my darkness for light and literally transformed me in the process. I let go of everything, even the secret I'd clung to for so long. So here it comes. Are you ready?

I was a battered woman.

No, I didn't have a drug problem or live in poverty as stereotypes might suggest. My husband was not a whiskey-swilling slob. We were a middle-class Christian family. As man and wife, we volunteered with the youth group, participated in couples' Bible studies, and attended marriage conferences. We took part in service projects and short-term missions.

From all outward appearances, we enjoyed a loving, godly marriage. But when church services ended, when we said goodbye to our friends and shut tight the doors of our private home, things were very, very different.

Terrifying.

Confusing.

Unpredictable.

No one ever walks down the aisle thinking, *I can't wait to begin my new life as a battered wife. Being intimidated and controlled is going to be amazing! I am so excited to live in fear and shame!* I approached my handsome groom with the same hopes and dreams all youthful brides share. Love, joy, companionship, and happy children. From the moment I met my husband, I wholeheartedly believed these things would be mine. I also walked down the aisle carrying some "baggage," as most of us do. Mine consisted of false beliefs about myself and God. For some reason, I had long believed that God was frequently displeased with me and watching for a reason to send me to hell. I thought I was inherently flawed, unworthy of love, and unable to measure up. So I worked to earn his love and favor by being good.

I have lived and died by the affirmation or criticism of others. Fearing rejection, I expended a lot of energy trying to be liked by everyone and loved by God. Until now, I kept these beliefs to myself. It's embarrassing and socially unacceptable to confess our inadequacies. Healthy people are happy and secure, right?

I'm no longer so sure about that, and I wonder if perhaps you might struggle with some of the same things I do.

And heck, if God can give me the strength not only to face the truth about my life but also to share that truth with others, I might as well come clean. I have a sneaking suspicion my false beliefs had a lot to do with how I ended up in abuse, and why I stayed so long. But now I'm open to the healing of the Holy Spirit, and I continue to gain more insight into these things. In the process, I'm becoming whole and healed.

For twenty-two years, I prayed God would change my husband's behavior and put an end to his violence toward me. The prayer went unanswered, and God became very small to me. So small, in fact, that when my husband threatened to kill me, I purchased extra life insurance, made out a will, and resigned to a violent death at his hands.

But today as I look back, remarkable events have taken place. What God has done both for me and in me is truly miraculous, and I will literally burst if I don't share the story! So confident was I in the power and might of my great God that I began this book even while my situation wasn't resolved. I literally had no idea in what way my salvation was coming. But at some point, I knew with absolute certainty that it was.

"Who among you fears the LORD and obeys the word of his servant?" says Isaiah 50:10. "Let the one who walks in the dark, who has no light, trust in the name of the LORD and rely on their God." I have always feared the Lord, and more than anything I desire to obey Christ. I was walking in the dark for a very long time, and although I didn't yet see the light, I could feel it.

On average, four women are killed every day in the United States by their spouses or boyfriends.[1] I'm here to tell my story of survival because I gripped Jesus' hand and trusted him to lead me to safety. I pray that the insights I've gained through my journey will help others living a similar nightmare.

So now, deep breath. I'll start at the beginning.

1

DARKNESS

I met Chad at church. He was ten years older than my nineteen, and for me it was love at first sight. Chad was experienced and successful, and he opened my eyes to a big, new, wonderful world.

Where my idea of fine dining was an occasional trip to Sizzler for Steak and Malibu Chicken, Chad treated me to elegant dinners at romantic seaside restaurants. He even bought me cute outfits to wear for our nights on the town. Before meeting Chad, my only experience with musical theatre was a trip to Los Angeles with my cousins when I was twelve to see *Annie*. Chad purchased the best seats in the house for all the award-winning shows. *Phantom of the Opera. Les Misérables.* If the show was acclaimed, we were there. Gift-giving was his specialty. Flowers, homemade cards, clothing. Every time he showered me with another token of his love and affection, I had to pinch myself. Was this a dream?

And there was more, the icing on the cake. He was a Christian. I had been praying for a godly husband ever since I was a little girl, and Chad seemed to love God as much as I did. He eagerly assumed the role of spiritual leader in our relationship. He answered my questions about theology, and we prayed together daily. He led us in devotions, and I grew in awe of his knowledge of the Bible.

After dating for only a couple of months, I knew I wanted to spend the rest of my life with Chad. He was my very first love, and I hoped and prayed he felt the way I did.

"This has been up here for a couple of years," he told me, as he removed a white envelope that had been pinned to a corkboard in his room. I noticed the envelope was marked with the word "saver," as he took his place beside me on the floor. "I know we have only been dating for two months, but I want to show you what's inside." He opened the envelope and pulled out a stunning antique wedding ring set of white gold. Petite diamonds encircled the band, and the engagement ring was square cut, simple, and elegant. It was perfect for me.

"We can buy you a new set if you don't like this one. But this ring belonged to my grandmother, and if you like it, I want you to have it someday." Chad loved me just as much as I loved him! This was a dream come true. We kept this moment to ourselves and continued to date, get to know each other, and make plans for the future.

During our fourteen-month courtship, I fell in love with an incredibly thoughtful, caring, and sweet man. Once, while I was studying at my college library, Chad surprised me with a visit. With an array of my favorite snacks in hand, he sat beside me while I studied. Another time, I went to see him after having an argument with my parents, and he held me while I cried. He listened attentively. He made little origami hearts out of tissue. He brightened my boring days at work, arriving unexpectedly with a bouquet of wild flowers or a thoughtful note expressing his admiration for me.

"You are beautiful," he would write. "You are smarter than I will ever be. I am so lucky to have you. You are the best thing that ever happened to me." Ninety-nine percent of the time, Chad was amazing and supportive. It was the other one percent I should have paid attention to.

Not long after we started dating, Chad confessed that only two months prior to meeting me he had broken up with a serious girlfriend. He had considered marrying her until he found out she had genital herpes and knew she wasn't the woman of his dreams. He had kept himself pure and was looking for someone who had also kept themselves pure. Inside, I beamed with pride. *Thank God I'm a virgin and still in the running for the "Woman of Chad's Dreams" award!*

But then he went on about how angry he had been with God for "taking her away from me. I cursed him out loud right here in this very room," he shared. "I was flipping him off and calling him the F-word over and over again. I told him I hated him." Only later would it occur to me that God hadn't taken anyone away from Chad. The girl didn't break up with Chad. He broke up with her. Everyone makes mistakes, and there are wonderful Christian wives and husbands who have made a mistake in the past and had to deal with a sexually transmitted disease. But at the time I was just thankful that I'd kept myself pure and could please Chad in this way.

There was more. "I was so heart-broken," he said, "I tried to kill myself. I had a gun in my mouth. I wanted to pull the trigger so badly, but I was too big of a wuss. I'm such a loser—I couldn't even kill myself!"

Instead of hearing alarm bells, I cried as I listened and felt sorry for Chad. He had suffered so much! I just wanted to make things better for him.

On one of our dates, while we waited in line at a local drive-thru, three young men goofed around in a convertible behind us on a warm and sunny Southern California day. The boys' fun time came to an abrupt halt when Chad became convinced they were "looking at" me and approached their vehicle. "You guys have something you want to say to me?" he screamed, leaning into their vehicle and pounding his fist on the windshield.

The driver backed away from Chad and raised his hands in a gesture of surrender. "Dude. We've got no problem with you."

Chad's face burned bright red and he shook with anger. "You better learn to keep your mouth shut, or someone is going to get hurt!" He pushed off of their car and stormed back to ours, keeping his eyes narrowed at the driver. His behavior made me feel special and loved. *Wow*, I thought, *this guy really loves me.*

A year later, on a beautiful day, we made our vows to one another in front of God, our families, and friends. Vows to love, honor, and cherish.

Shortly after we married, the ninety-nine to one-percent ratio changed to about fifty-fifty. My thoughtful, caring Chad shared residence with a critical and moody Chad. As I continued studying to become a nurse, both personalities might manifest themselves at any time on any given day. "Why are you wearing *that*?" Chad might say. Or "I will never understand how you can get straight As in all your classes and yet have no common sense." Or "I have an idea—why don't you actually think for once!"

Other times when I dialed his office, he would answer right away with "Hey you. It's good to hear your voice. How are you?"

"I'm making pasta tonight," I'd say while I busily chopped veggies for a salad. "Do you want Alfredo sauce, marinara, or both?"

"You know me. I'm easy. Whatever you like. Hey, I love you very much. I want to make sure you always know that."

Thirty minutes later, when I'd call back to ask him to stop for parmesan cheese on the way home, he would roar, "What's the problem?!"

"Have I done something to upset you? Has something happened?"

"No! Just back off! Man, what is your deal?"

Anxiety would cause my hands to tremble as I set the table. My mind would spin. *I must have done something to make him angry. But what? What is he going to be like when he gets home? How can I make things better?*

The gate would bellow its signature creaking as he stepped into our patio. I'd brace myself for the worst. But he'd just breeze through the front door with a smile, a "Hey you," and a kiss on the cheek. "Dinner smells good. You look pretty."

So very confusing.

While the mood swings were difficult, they were the least of my problems. Only weeks after we made vows to one another, alarming behaviors appeared. If I expressed any negative emotion, such as sadness or hurt feelings over something he said, he would go off. And then I'd be punished for making him feel so awful about himself. When this happened while we were driving, I was especially terrified.

Once, when he asked why I was so quiet, I answered truthfully that I was sad because he had yelled at me.

"Oh, really? So this is all my fault? I am so sick and tired of being the bad guy! I guess I am just a piece of s***!" He slammed the accelerator to the floor until I dug my nails into the sides of my seat. "Please don't," I pleaded, as tears began to roll and fear overwhelmed me.

Suddenly we were flying down a residential street at seventy miles per hour, against my will. "Please stop!" My plea fell on deaf ears. I held my breath as we gained on the little black Toyota directly in front of us that was traveling at the speed limit until a collision seemed inevitable. *Screech!* The right side of my body pressed forcefully into the passenger door as we swerved around the car. A second later, my left side was pressed into Chad as he jerked the wheel back to center. He glanced at me and laughed.

"Please stop. You are scaring me." But he just pushed the pedal to the metal and turned the wheel to the right, steering the car closer and closer to the sidewalk. "Is this what you want?" We were now less than two feet away from a telephone pole. "No. I'm sorry. Please stop!" He returned the car to center and jammed his foot on the brake, skidding to a violent stop. The seat belt cut into my chest. I covered my face with my hands and sobbed all the way home.

Neither was it safe to relay any sort of negative information at home. Chad began to self-mutilate in front of me whenever I expressed concern over our relationship, insisting it was my fault that he was doing such terrifying things. "It makes me feel bad when you yell at me," I said once.

Chad grabbed a knife out of the butcher block. I watched in horror as he pretended to plunge the blade into his abdomen, chest, and head over and over again. "Is this what you want?! Do you like making me feel this way?"

I dropped to my knees and begged him to stop. A few weeks later, it happened again. He asked me, "Why are you crying?"

Don't say it, Jenny. Whatever you do, don't answer that question.

"Please tell me. I love you. How can I know what's going on with you if you won't talk to me?"

He seems to really want to know. How can he be the husband he should be if I am not honest with him? Maybe things will be different this time. "Well, it hurts my feelings when you put me down."

The look on Chad's face told me this time was not going to be any different. He went to the closet, returned with the iron, and hit himself on the side of the head repeatedly while I wept and prayed for him to stop.

I learned to keep my mouth shut about anything he might perceive as criticism. Still, even my best efforts could not always prevent an outburst. Suddenly a coffee cup was whizzing past my head, or the entire contents of the kitchen counter cleared with one violent swoop of his arm.

He became unreasonably protective of me and often raged when another man dared look my way. No longer did his jealousy make me feel special. Now that his aggressive behavior was aimed toward me, I felt intimidated and afraid.

Flinging coffee cups and punching walls were one thing, but firearms were another. Soon after we were married, Chad informed me that he did not feel he could adequately protect us without a firearm, and he purchased his first gun. I say "first" because that purchase led to many. Soon he had a stockpile of weapons. He carried a notebook in which he'd write down the license plate numbers of suspicious-looking cars and descriptions of suspicious-looking people. It was his job to keep me safe, he insisted. And the only way he could protect me was to carry a firearm on his person at all times. Whether out of the house or in, my new husband was now armed with a loaded weapon twenty-four hours per day.

Needless to say, married life was not what I had imagined. I frequently experienced terrifying nightmares and often awoke screaming in the middle of the night, my body dripping in sweat. I developed chronic stomach-aches and chest pains. I felt uneasy, afraid, and confused. And I cried a lot. But crying in front of Chad would lead to one of his emotional meltdowns, so I cried in isolation.

My relationship with my family became strained. During our court-ship, and especially after we married, Chad convinced me they were bad and that staying away from them was best for all of us. Only a few months into married life, Chad noticed that his new bride had been completely overtaken by sadness. He told me I was most likely experiencing this sadness because my "dysfunctional" family was mistreating me. He supported me in my decision to go to counseling.

2

WHAT A MONSTER LOOKS LIKE

*M*y counselor had tender eyes and her demeanor was sweet and calm. During our first meeting, she took a patient history.

Describe your life at home when you were a child.

Have you been a victim of sexual abuse?

What is your relationship with your siblings like?

How would you describe your dad?

I was able to relay a painful memory while feeling absolutely nothing. She stopped me as I spoke. "What you are telling me is very painful. How does it make you feel as you tell this story?"

Nothing. I felt absolutely nothing. No sadness, no anger, no feeling at all. I'd blunted myself from experiencing pain. She pointed out in a kind way that my response was not exactly healthy, and for several sessions we hashed through some of the things I had endured as a child. But truthfully, I wasn't yet ready to deal with them. Even though I didn't volunteer any information about what was going on in my home, she must have known something was wrong. As the weeks went by, she questioned me more and more about my life as a new bride.

She slowly gained my trust, and I started to share my horror stories. I offered only generalizations at first. "I know he really loves me, and he's a wonderful person, but sometimes he gets really mad and it's kind of scary."

"What does scary look like?" she'd ask. At first I confessed the less terrifying things—flying objects, mood swings. She listened intently, silently taking notes. She looked at me with compassion and concern, and my ability to block out the pain failed. Tears started flowing. Eventually I told the whole truth. About hiding in the bathtub. Being backed into corners. The reckless driving and self-mutilation.

During each session I recalled a different nightmare in horrifying detail, and although her face remained neutral, the big, beautiful eyes staring back at me gave her true feelings away—she was deeply concerned for me. And then I told her about the guns.

Usually she did more questioning and listening than speaking. But when she found out Chad was armed, everything changed. "You are not safe. This is not normal. You are being abused." My head was ringing as she spoke. My heart was pounding. I tried desperately to wrap my mind around what she was saying. Still with tenderness and concern, but now also with fear and urgency, she tried to help me see my situation as it really was. "I know that you love him, but love shouldn't hurt like this. He is hurting you. He isn't showing you love when he puts your life in danger. I'm pleading with you. You must leave this relationship for your safety."

I came close to fainting when she finally said what needed to be said. Staring straight ahead, I tried to keep from hyperventilating. Tears stained my cheeks as she looked at me with such tenderness, such compassion that even thinking about it years later still moves me deeply. I drove home from counseling and wept so hard I vomited. I laid on the couch and for a long time pondered her words. Then I made my decision. I knew better than her.

She didn't know Chad like I did! If only I loved him like no one else had ever loved him, he would be healed. He just needed to improve his self-esteem, and I was the only person on the planet who could save him. That was the beginning of the end of my time in counseling. At twenty years of age, despite being offered a way of escape, I chose to stay in the darkness.

Meanwhile, Chad and I repeated the same behaviors over and over. I was cognizant that our negative interactions followed a somewhat predictable pattern, despite my efforts to stop them from occurring.

For one, I mastered the art of walking on eggshells, even adopting a theme song to the tune of Katrina and the Waves' hit "Walking on Sunshine."[1] My version of the cheerful tune went, "I'm walking on eggshells, oh yeah. And it's startin' to feel bad!" The song became my mantra during those cycles when, without explanation, Chad's mood became increasingly depressed and he spent most of his free time on the couch brooding. At first I tried gentle words of understanding. "Is everything all right?" I'd ask, taking hold of his hand.

"Everything's fine," he'd respond, in a monotone voice, staring off into nowhere. Further questioning led to further withdrawal or a curt reply. A thick cloud of tension was building again. When he left the house for work, I breathed a sigh of relief, and when he returned I expended tremendous amounts of energy trying to read him and respond appropriately.

He's angry about something. I'd better keep my distance.

He seems sad. Maybe I should console him.

He isn't happy with me. I should go on a diet and start exercising more.

I guarded my tongue, evaded his glances, changed my diet, and braced myself for the inevitable outburst.

Sure enough, all the energy I'd expended would prove a waste. No amount of tip-toeing, passivity, or self-improvement could prevent what came next. "What is that supposed to mean?" Chad might respond to an innocent remark. With his loaded question, I knew I was in for it.

"I didn't mean anything bad. I'm sorry." I'd wave a white flag of surrender.

"You're sorry? Do you have any idea how hard I work for you? If you have a problem with me, then let's get it out. Right here, right now!" If I responded with tears, Chad called himself names, threatened suicide, or self-mutilated. I'd stop crying, apologize for causing him pain, and beg him not to follow through with his threat to kill himself.

If I responded by fighting back, things were worse. "I have done nothing wrong!" I'd scream, succumbing to my rising anger.

"Do you really want to take me on? I don't think so!" He'd press his body against me and push his face into mine while backing me up against the wall. "Want me to show you what a monster looks like?" He'd shake his fist above my head. I'd drop to the ground, pull my knees into my chest, and cry tears of fear and shame.

"Oh please, you're so dramatic! I have never hurt you once!" To get his point across, there might come a *swoosh!* and then a *crash!* as he sent plates and utensils flying off the counter and through the air. I'd wince and duck for cover, praying for the nightmare to end. During one particularly violent fight, he pressed me backward until I was in our bedroom and sent me tumbling onto our bed. He left me there, sobbing in despair. *Oh good. Maybe it's over.* But moments later he returned. I looked up from my crying to see him standing over me with a baseball bat raised above his head. *Oh God, this is it! He's really going to kill me!*

My entire body quivered with terror. *Whack!* The bat came crashing down an inch from my head. One whack apparently wasn't enough to teach me a lesson. I squeezed my eyes tight. *Boom!* Another brutal blow shook the bed. Chad's chest heaved in and out. His face was crimson. He threw the bat to the ground and left. For a long time, I just laid there and stared off into nowhere. Numb. Terrified. Alone. Confused.

During the early years of our marriage, what followed was a heartfelt, tearful apology accompanied by a promise to change. "I never meant to hurt you," he would say. "I love you so much, and if I had known I was like this, I never would have married you or anyone else. I'll do anything to make it right." Then came a persuasive declaration of his desperate need for me. "I'm so lucky to have you. I can't believe you love me. I couldn't survive without you." And we'd both vow to love each other better. I felt extremely close to him in these moments and gained a sense of importance and purpose. *I'm the one person on the planet who loves him so completely.* Being his only rescuer made me strengthen my resolve to love him to complete healing.

But as the years progressed, the apology phase morphed into something completely different. There was no more remorse from Chad. No tears. No promises to change. Flowers still appeared on the kitchen table, but they were "just because." His new response could be summed up in one word, *denial*. Chad acted as if nothing had happened. While I lay in a heap on the floor, recovering from the latest assault, Chad merrily went about his business. Any attempt I made to discuss the incident was dismissed. "I thought everything was fine," he might say.

For a while, things would settle down, and we would simply tend to the business of life. We said "I love you" every day, and we went out to eat and to the movies like normal couples. I worked part-time as a nursing assistant, did the laundry, and hoped that things would be different. Sometimes this time of peace and calm lasted only a week, and sometimes it lasted a few months. But always, eventually, tension began once again to build, and the whole hellish cycle repeated itself. I was living in a nightmare.

3

WIFE AS ACCOMPLICE

*G*od must have known I was going to stay.

Six months into our marriage, I attended a women's retreat through our church, made small talk with the other ladies, and did my best to fit in and pretend everything was fine. But secretly I was overwhelmed with sorrow. Early one morning, I hiked alone to a quiet wooded area and found a small clearing in which to sit. I leaned against a rugged old tree, pulled my knees into my chest, and sobbed. *Father, I'm so sad. So confused. Lost. Please help me. Please heal Chad. I don't want to live like this anymore.*

The Spirit of God had spoken to me on numerous occasions in my life prior to this communion in the woods. I had learned to discern his voice—not in an audible way, but rather a voice I could hear in my spirit. Again this day, a soft yet distinct voice spoke right to the very core of my being, as if my heart had ears. "It is not going to get any easier. But I will be with you."

This wasn't what I wanted to hear, but I knew it was from him. I even shared my revelation with the group, although I didn't dare tell anyone what was going on inside my home. I had only told one person about my situation, the counselor, and had rejected the support she offered. I hadn't told my family or friends.

Instead, I plunged headfirst into "healing" my husband. And I went along with the charade he put on in public. Chad was showy with his affection for me, especially immediately following a violent episode. Many times at work I was forced to muddle through my day with a foggy mind, trying desperately to push away the disturbing scene of the night before replaying in my head. And while I agonized over what things might be like when I returned home, Chad would waltz into my place of work with a warm smile and a gorgeous bouquet of flowers. My co-workers would melt and say, "You're so lucky!"

And so I lived a double life. In private, I prayed, cried, and fasted. I pled with Chad to change. I was an intelligent woman with a good job, ashamed of the behavior I was tolerating. But I couldn't bear to think how my friends and co-workers would perceive me if they knew how often I hid in my bathtub, shaking uncontrollably with fear. So in public I was Chad's number-one accomplice in his attempts to convince everyone what a loving and supportive husband I had.

As the violence continued, I began to believe that Chad's public image must be his true self, and what was happening to me in private was due to some defect of my own. He was creative and funny. He was well liked. He had a heart for giving and appeared to genuinely enjoy helping people. He was especially sweet to older folks and always willing to lend a hand to a friend in need. He seemed to enjoy doing things to make me feel loved and often said that he bragged about me. All this added to my confusion.

How could he act genuinely happy and carefree, and then, in a flash, turn into a completely different person? How could he treat others so differently than he treated me behind closed doors? His mistreatment of me alone strengthened my belief that I was the defective one.

Perhaps I was hysterical for no reason. Perhaps Chad was right; I was overly sensitive.

Sometimes, immediately after a volatile episode, I would have to pull myself together and put a smile on my face to attend a family function. When Chad told a joke at my expense, I endured everyone's laughter.

When I couldn't find the strength to join in their laughter, Chad rolled his eyes and gave his *overly sensitive* wife a hug, kissed me on the cheek, and said, "I was just kidding, and everyone knows it but you." And in that moment, everyone could see how overly sensitive I was indeed.

For a while, he even skillfully convinced my sister, Holly, that I was a lazy, ungrateful wife.

"I can't take this anymore," I cried on the phone one day, when I finally got the courage to reach out to her. I wasn't aware Chad had already spoken with her. When I wasn't around, Chad had been pouring out his heart to her, telling her how hard he worked to be patient with me. As frustrating as it was, he told her, he was dedicated. He would not give up on me.

When Holly arrived at my home, I came out of my bedroom with eyes red and swollen from crying and a broken heart. "He works so hard for you, and you just don't appreciate it." I couldn't believe my ears. "You're so sensitive, and you make a big deal about everything. I see it, Jenny, how he does everything around here and you do nothing. You need to stop being a brat."

I wanted to die. Literally. Even my sister didn't believe me, instead siding with Chad. I was truly alone in the world. The pain and rejection was too much.

Holly didn't know I was being battered, that I spent my nights crying and begging God to take my life. That the reason I spent much of my free time sleeping was because I was morbidly depressed. Or that he was also playing the other side, craftily relaying any mean things Holly said about me. "You can't trust her like you think you can," he would say with concern. "I know how much you love your sister, and it hurts me to have to be the one to tell you this, but she really puts you down when we talk. I love you though, and I'm on your side. You will always have me."

Using similar tactics, Chad had already been successful in isolating me from my parents. But my bond with my sister proved a tough nut for him to crack. Shortly after this incident, she came to her senses and realized she had been deceived. Throughout the years she had witnessed tiny glimpses of the hell I was enduring. Eventually Chad's manipulative tricks were overpowered by our sisterhood. Although he'd managed to convince me that my parents didn't really love me, he was unable to break the bond between my sister and me.

Now and again, I asserted myself. One evening, after we had been married for a couple of years, we returned to our little apartment after a tense night out, and I just wanted to go to bed. But Chad started in. Like it or not, I was going to be involved in yet another altercation. "I'm so tired," I said, rubbing my temples and walking toward the bedroom. "Can we just do this tomorrow?"

His hand gripped my arm. "You don't walk away from me when I am talking to you!"

I was so exhausted, my head ached, and I was teetering on the edge of my breaking point. The thought of enduring yet another tirade was too much. Instead of submitting, I tried to pull away. His grip tightened. "Let me go!" I begged, as the tears started to roll.

He released me and began ranting while banging his head against the wall. One blow after the other. *Bang! Bang! Bang!* "Why do you always do this to me? I would give my life for you." *Bang! Bang!* "All I want is for you to be happy. Why can't you see that? You treat me like some kind of monster!" *Bang! Bang! Bang!* In that moment, all the craziness, all my hopelessness, all the terror and confusion came rushing at me. I sank to the ground and wept uncontrollably, while Chad screamed obscenities over me. But this time he wasn't calling me names. He was alternately calling himself every four-letter word in the book and then raging against me for making him feel bad about himself. Then he turned his back to me and pulled his buttocks apart. "I am so sick and tired of getting screwed by everyone!" I shut my eyes tight and begged God to take away the pain. "Please, God. Please, God. Please!" I repeated my desperate prayer until my sobbing turned into hyperventilation, and I was able to completely block Chad out. I lay in that state for I don't know how long, while somewhere, seemingly far away, dishes crashed against the kitchen floor.

"Jenny." Chad's voice was coming from our bedroom down the hall. I could see him sitting on the edge of the bed, shoulders now relaxed, elbows resting on his knees. "Can we please just talk?"

Using my shirt to wipe the tears, I made my way to the bedroom. I sat on the floor, numb. "I can't do this anymore. It hurts too much." For once, he listened. But then things took a nightmarish turn.

"I'm sorry you're hurting so bad. I am too. There is something we can do about it." I didn't understand what he meant. Then he reached between the mattress and box spring. My breath caught. He was holding a loaded hand gun.

Chad gripped the powerful weapon with both hands. "This ends now. After tonight, you won't feel any pain."

I had endured countless moments of terror before, but this eclipsed them all. A cloud of darkness and dread filled the tiny room. Despite all the times I had prayed for God to take my life, I knew I wasn't ready to die. I hesitated.

"Just do it," he said, placing the gun by my hand. "You don't have to feel any more pain. You can end it right now. Just do it."

My body trembled. My heart hammered. I stared at the weapon. *I can't shoot myself. I don't want to shoot myself.* My palms were drenched in sweat. I rubbed them on my jeans. I shook my head no.

But in that moment, he won. I had got the message, loud and clear. I needed to shut up. No more expressing my agony. No more tears. To stay alive, I'd have to suck it up. Keep my suffering to myself.

Chad tucked the gun away, said goodnight, and drifted off into what appeared to be a peaceful slumber. Meanwhile, I lay awake, staring at the ceiling, questioning God. *Why haven't you answered my prayers for Chad's healing? Why do you allow me to suffer? Are you even listening? I thought you loved me.*

4

A FALSE PEACE

For the first time, I seriously entertained the thought of leaving my husband.

Run!

But what would my family think? I couldn't imagine admitting that my husband had just attempted to convince me to shoot myself. This was too humiliating. *I'm so ashamed.* Who would even believe Chad was capable of something like that?

Run to a shelter, a neighbor, or a friend. I heard the urgent whisper in my spirit. *Get up now and run!*

But what about God? "God hates divorce." I'd heard this mantra over and over, and it tortured me. Our pastor had just given a sermon on love. According to the Bible, love *always* hopes, love doesn't keep a record of wrongs, and love *never fails*. And I made vows to Chad. In sickness and in health. Chad was definitely very sick. There was no way out. I had to stay and learn to love Chad perfectly—just like the Bible said.

This was my cross to bear.

Still, I knew that Chad's behavior was wrong. Something had to change, or I was going to end up dead. In the morning over breakfast, I told Chad I loved him very much, but that he was very ill. He needed help, and I wasn't going to rest until he got it. He cried and thanked me for loving him so completely. He promised he'd do anything I asked, to make things right. I was so relieved. *Things are going to be just fine after all.* Only they weren't.

Chad humbly agreed to go to anger management classes. I did some research and found a group that met at a local church. The night of his first meeting he left the house with his Bible in hand. As he waved good-bye, I was elated. Finally he was going to change.

"Those guys are all a bunch of nut jobs!" he hissed, as he blew through the front door. "One idiot was even talking to himself. I don't belong there." No more anger management for Chad.

We repeated this cycle numerous times. "I will do anything you ask," led to a one-day commitment to reading his Bible. Or one class, or one counseling appointment.

Sometime after our third anniversary, my gynecologist informed me that my pap smear was abnormal. I had contracted *human papillomavirus* or HPV—the kind of genital warts that cause cervical cancer. Research revealed that it takes exactly three years from exposure to see cervical changes on a pap smear. This dangerous strain does not manifest any symptoms in the male. God knows, I had never been in a sexual relationship with anyone but Chad. So that whole "I have kept myself pure" was a whopper of a lie, and I was now paying the price. As a result, I had to go under general anesthesia and have surgery.

Chad and I had been married for seven years when I finally reached my breaking point. I wrote him a letter telling him so, and this time I was serious. I'd resigned myself to living out the rest of my life in isolation, as a eunuch. Childless and alone. Anything was better than living this way. I was done.

Dear Chad,

I can't do this anymore. I keep begging you to change but you don't. You are hurting me and I can't live like this. I am going to talk with our pastor about seeking a legal separation. I have told you over and over again that if you keep treating me this way I am going to leave, and now I'm ready. You obviously don't love me because you won't stop hurting me. I'm sorry, but there is nothing else I can do.

By twenty-seven years old, I had prayed countless times in earnest for Chad to be healed. For his behavior to change. When that prayer went unanswered, I prayed for my own death. Cancer. A car crash. Whatever. *I don't care, Lord. Just please let me die.*

I never prayed for rescue. I never prayed for deliverance. It never occurred to me that Jesus was willing to save me from the abuse. Or that Chad's behavior was a total affront to my heavenly Father. If I had to go on living, I needed to separate from Chad. A legal separation was the only answer.

Chad gripped the letter. "I can't believe this." He stared at the carpet for a long time. "A legal separation? You can't be serious. There has to be another way. I am so sorry. I know I have hurt you over and over again, but you have to give me another chance. This time will be different. I promise. I know I need help. Professional help. I swear to you that I will get the help I need." This time he followed through on his promise.

Chad went to counseling right away and he stayed in counseling. He confessed his self-loathing and his depression. He confessed that he felt like he never measured up. He confessed that he was a bad communicator and hard to live with. He confessed a lot of things. But he never confessed his abuse. The counselor even had me sit in on a few sessions during which Chad cried bitter tears and spoke of the self-hatred he lived with every day. I felt sorry for him. No wonder he treated me so badly.

The counselor never asked if I was being abused. He never asked if Chad had an anger problem. But after several months, the counselor determined that Chad's mental health issues were too big for talk therapy only. "I'm not exactly sure what kind personality disorder your husband has," he said. "But his issues are beyond me. He needs a psychiatrist." I listened politely and thanked him. The fact that Chad had a serious mental problem didn't surprise me. And there was good news in the counselor's findings. Chad could take medicine. Finally, things were going to change.

The psychiatrist never asked to meet with me, but she did start Chad on a medication, and within three weeks his behavior drastically improved. His mood was stable, and he seemed much happier. I was so grateful for the medication and the long-overdue changes in Chad. I forgot all about the legal separation, and we moved forward together.

Just when I started to believe the drug was a magical answer to all our problems, pre-medicated-Chad behavior started popping up in medicated Chad. The violent behaviors returned, revealing the truth—mental illness and abuse are two separate issues. Where I had once believed that mental illness explained and excused abuse, I now realized I was mistaken. The abusive behaviors returned despite Chad's stabilized mood. He screamed. He threw things. He intimidated and devalued me. He drove like a lunatic when I made him angry. The only difference was that he was more stable between outbursts. Unfortunately, by the time I figured all this out, I had given birth to our first child.

The good news was that Chad genuinely seemed to enjoy being a father. He held our son tenderly and rocked him to sleep. He changed diapers, played peek-a-boo, and thanked me for giving him a son. Things weren't perfect by any means, but being a mother was a healing balm to my heart. Having a child united us, and often we were too busy to argue. Six months later, all that changed. "What day of your cycle are you on?" my sister asked. She knew I'd been waiting for my period to arrive.

I looked at the calendar. "Day fifty-one."

"There is no day fifty-one, silly! Just take a pregnancy test."

My six-month-old toddled around in the bathroom while I peed on the stick. Within five seconds, the pink plus-sign popped up. I felt dizzy. Holly peeked her head in. "Well?" I showed her the stick, and we started laughing. I looked down at my baby slobbering all over my foot and shook my head. I should have felt panic, but I just felt joy.

"How are you going to tell Chad?" I didn't waste any time. Holly stayed with the baby while I put the stick in a plastic bag and headed straight for Chad's office.

He stared at the stick for a long time. "All I can say is this must be God's will, because not twenty-four hours ago I was trying to decide how to tell you I wanted a vasectomy."

Whew. That was a close one. I thanked the Lord for allowing me to get pregnant again. Whenever we were in public, Chad acted like having another child was a blessing. But for the entire nine-month pregnancy, I got the silent treatment. The moment I gave birth to our second son, all was well between us again. Chad pretended his gestational grudge had never happened.

Being a mom was the best thing that ever happened to me. I enjoyed every second of the infant phase and adored the toddler phase. Having preschoolers was amazing, and don't even get me started about grade school. I threw myself into motherhood, and for the first time experienced true love. I loved my kids with all my heart and Chad took notice. "You sure spend a lot of time with the boys. I still exist, you know," he would say. Although Chad enjoyed being a dad, he frequently talked about how nice it was going to be when the kids were grown and living their own lives. Then it would just be the two of us again.

I tried not to think about it.

I am ashamed to admit that Chad and I often fought in front of our two small boys. He managed to control his behavior around them for the most part, which shocked me. So he wasn't totally unable to control his violent outbursts? Nevertheless, the same old ugly tension hung around our home, along with the vile cycle of abuse. Only now there were children in the mix who were growing old enough to notice that bad things were happening. But being a mom awakened a new courage in me. I never tolerated any bad behavior toward our kids. If I discerned even a whiff of inappropriate anger, I came running—claws out and ready for battle.

One evening, I heard Chad screaming at the top of his lungs. "You boys get in here right now!" I tossed the laundry aside and sprinted to the living room.

"What's the problem?" My face was red, and I was ready to pounce. My sons, six and seven at the time, stood at attention, looking scared.

Chad glared at me with disdain. "You stay out of this! They're being disrespectful and I'm not going to tolerate it! Do you understand me?" He jabbed an angry finger toward their confused little faces.

Rage engulfed me like a swarm of hornets. "Back off! They're just kids, and they're *good* kids!" I stepped between Chad and the boys. "You leave them alone!"

Clang! The burners from the stove sailed through the air. *Crash!* One of them struck the sliding glass door. The boys started crying. "Get out of this house now!" I screamed, heart pounding. For the first time in my life, I felt that I could physically inflict harm on someone. I hated Chad in that moment.

"You want me to leave?" he spat. He fisted his hands and gritted his teeth.

"Yes! I want you to leave this house. Get out now!" Finally I was standing up to my abuser. And then . . . both of my young sons ran toward Chad.

They clung to him, one attached to each leg. "No, Dad. Don't leave!"

I was stunned. Chad relaxed. "It's all right," he said. "Dad's not going anywhere." Then the three men in my life walked hand in hand and lay down together on my bed.

I sat in my car, in the darkness, and wept. "Dear God, I need you. I have brought children into a horrific situation and I don't know what to do. They want their dad . . ." Gripping the steering wheel, I lay my head down and continued to weep. "Please, you have to help me. I have made children with a maniac, and now I'm lost."

He answered me in an instant. *You must keep peace for your children. Leave Chad to me. He is not your responsibility. Lean into me. Let me be your husband. I will meet all your needs.*

I wiped my tears, took a deep breath, and walked back into my abusive home.

No Peace Within

I plunged headfirst into my mission—keep the peace. When Chad started to rant, I remained silent. No tears. No anger. No rebuttal. I became an expert at bait recognition—discerning when he was reeling me into a fight. When I sensed he was looking for a reason to explode, I did not take the bait.

Chad controlled all of our finances. I just accepted this. He installed a baby monitor, allegedly for the purposes of listening for the doorbell or phone to ring when he was in his office. But if he overheard a conversation of which he disapproved, he reprimanded me. I took his rebuke and said nothing.

A few benefits occurred as a result of my new mission. Peace did come to our home. The fighting stopped. Things were more stable for our children, which meant the world to me. But some negative consequences emerged as well. As I became more passive outwardly, an inner rage began to fill me. I felt like a slave who had no real freedom yet pretended to appreciate their master so as not to be punished. Once or twice a year, I would break down and hit Chad with six months of pent-up fury. "I hate you so much! I wish I never had to lay eyes on you again!" And if I really wanted to hit him below the belt, when he wasn't looking I'd raise both of my middle fingers and wave them wildly in his direction.

As I surrendered my rights and my will to his control, any feelings of closeness and love evaporated. Only fear and hate remained. I manufactured a happy face for outsiders, but in private I was desperately defeated. Sad. Hopeless. Despairing. Ashamed. Powerless.

As days, then months, then years passed, and my prayers still went unanswered, I spent less and less time with my Redeemer. Instead I coped by daydreaming, pretending I had an entirely different life. I often felt the Spirit calling me, drawing me to spend time with him, but I always found something else to do. Even when I ended my day with the Lord, by the time my head hit the pillow I was exhausted. After a few Bible verses and a couple of prayers, I'd drift off to sleep with thoughts of my fake Prince Charming sweeping me up in his arms and whisking me away from all my troubles—instead of allowing God to be my husband and meet my needs as he had promised. I didn't have affairs or drown myself in drugs and alcohol, but I numbed my mind with the sweet denial that comes with living in Fantasy Land instead of Real Land. Real Land was too painful, while Fantasy Land became a frequent safe haven.

Satan was also present. Whispering doubts. Slandering God.

You sure have been praying a long time. I guess God isn't really listening. Guess he isn't so good after all. You did everything right, and look how things turned out for you. All those years obeying God, and this is how he repays you? Interesting . . .

As I spent less time in the Word, I stopped combating the lies. My life of hell would never end. God was incapable of answering my prayers to heal Chad. That, or he refused. Either option left me defeated.

As I slid deeper into darkness and further from the light of God, I became judgmental of people who were getting a divorce. Especially women. I couldn't see it at the time, but I was feeding a powerful case of self-righteousness because of what I was tolerating. I became the world's biggest martyr. *How holy I am, able to stay in such a horrifying marriage!* Never mind that I was filled with hatred.

No doubt, the Devil was also heavily at work in Chad, feeding him a steady diet of lies as well. As time passed, there were no more tears or apologies. His disrespect of, and contempt for, me was palpable. His thinking became ever more darkened. His anger intensified.

We were no longer attending church, and it seemed Satan, that sly serpent, had won.

5

JUST A SPARK

Thankfully, God never gives up on us. No matter how far off track we get. No matter how deeply steeped in darkness we become.

Chad and I had not been a part of any church for quite some time, and the Spirit was pestering me about it. On a Sunday morning, I pulled the covers over my eyes to block the sunlight.

Draw near to me and I will draw near to you. I heard this in my spirit but ignored it.

Don't give up on church. I can minister to you there. I rolled over and decided to stay in bed.

This went on week after week. When it was apparent the Spirit was not going to stop sending me Sunday morning signals, I responded. It was time to listen to his voice. So I started a fast. My kids begged me to take them to McDonald's—really not the place to go when fasting. The smell of the french fries are enough to make even the most dedicated faster say to heck with it and order a super-size. But while the kids played in the ball pit, I folded my hands and placed them on top of the Bible I had brought along. *Lord, you had better do something if you want me to go to church. I'm so lost. So numb and cold. I know it's not your fault, but this is where I am at. If you want me to go to church so badly, you'll need to lead me.*

The prayer had barely passed through my lips when I was approached by a friendly young woman. "Hey," she said, "I remember your boys! I volunteer in the children's ministry at First Christian. They are so cute! My name is Sandy. It's nice to meet you." I remembered that we had visited her church just one time and that, on the way home, Chad and I tore it to shreds: "That music was super cheesy. I'm not so sure about that pastor. He seems pretty fake. I don't know, I just didn't like it."

Sandy joined me at my table as if we were old friends. "The ladies are just starting up a new Bible study on Wednesday mornings. I'd love it if you came. It will be really fun, and everyone is super nice."

I looked around and noted that the McDonald's was almost empty. Either she was talking to the homeless guy sitting in the booth next to us, or she was inviting *me*. I was taken off guard by her genuine spirit and friendliness. Clearly this was no coincidence, considering that I had just told God he needed to do something.

As crazy as it sounds, my liberation began during a fast at McDonald's. This intervention from the Lord would prove to be the first step on my journey out of the darkness.

This particular Bible study was about being freed from *strongholds*. In all my years as a Christian, I had never heard of such a thing. In simple terms, a stronghold is an entrenched pattern of thought, value, or behavior that is contrary to the Word and will of God.[1] It is a false belief that leads to bondage. For example, I would learn that my false belief that God was hard to please and looking for a reason to send me to hell led me to the bondage of legalism. Even though I was living a secret life of abuse, fear, shame, and pride, I hadn't been ready to face any of these things. The Spirit knew this. He also knew exactly which stronghold was keeping me from him and thus keeping me in the dark—daydreaming.

Our first assignment was to quiet ourselves before the Lord and ask him to speak to our Spirit and reveal any strongholds that needed to be brought down. "Dear Lord," I sighed deeply and then hesitated. It had been such a long time since I had entered into his presence. This was uncomfortable. But he waited patiently. "I am disappointed. Actually,

Lord, I'm disappointed with you. I know I'm not supposed to feel this way. But my life is hard. It's not at all what I expected. And even though I have been praying for Chad to be healed, nothing has happened. I guess I'm angry with you. I'm sorry. Anyway, thank you for reaching out to me through Sandy. Can you please show me what stronghold is keeping me from you?"

Right away, he brought to mind one of my go-to fantasies. A ruggedly handsome man with tanned skin, toned muscles, and beautiful eyes looks at me tenderly. We walk hand in hand along a pristine shore by a crystal-blue sea. He takes my face in his hands and kisses me tenderly. And then things get spicy. Oh shoot. "You mean I have to say goodbye to that guy?"

I filled an entire workbook with revelations and prayers that freed me from my addiction to daydreaming. "Addiction" may seem a strong word for such a silly thing, but I came to realize that I literally could not make it through my day without pretending I was someone else, somewhere else. The pretending prevented me from facing the truth—and it is the truth that sets us free.

When I finished the study, not one woman in the group had knowledge of what was going on in my home, but God had completed his intended work in me. I was no longer drifting off into Fantasy Land to ease my pain. I'd been forced to face the reality of my life and the depth of my pain, and I knew . . . I absolutely could not do this alone.

I needed Jesus.

6

FROM PIT TO PROVISION

*W*hen one is hashing out daily life as a battered wife, just trying to avoid every emotional and physical land mine, it's difficult to do more than simply survive. But slowly I discovered Chad had been telling me significant, ongoing lies, and they were beginning to have a radical impact on my life.

Although I'd been working full-time for quite a while, I wasn't allowed to have anything to do with our finances. Many times over I asked Chad to allow me to participate. If something happened to him, I reasoned, I would not even know how to pay the bills. He was always "too busy" or "needed time to get things organized before he could show me the ropes." It never happened.

When I started answering collection calls, I dared not cross Chad. But I knew I was capable and intelligent in all other areas of my life. So when the calls intensified, I gathered my courage and did some investigating. I discovered a notice from the city that our water was scheduled to be turned off for lack of payment. And there was more. My husband had accumulated eighty-five-thousand dollars of unsecured debt. Our credit was destroyed. I couldn't ignore this.

"I need to talk to you," I said.

Chad looked up only briefly from his computer. "It's going to have to wait."

I had been dismissed one too many times. "This can't wait." I confronted him with what I'd found. "Now I know why you put me off every time I asked you to show me the finances. You've been lying."

Picture the Incredible Hulk confined in a small garage full of boxes and tools, because that is the best way to adequately describe what happened next. *Crash! Whoosh! Clang! Zing!* Chad's face flamed red and he shook with rage as he heaved boxes and hammers and wrenches through the air. I assumed my usual duck-and-cover position. Too numb to shed a tear, I just walked away.

He never told me where all the money had gone, and I was too terrified to ask. Although we drove used cars, clipped coupons, and lived simply, somehow we were in seemingly insurmountable debt. And Chad's implication was clear—the debt I wasn't even aware of was all my fault. I silently went to work on getting a refinance. Fortunately, the value of our home had increased greatly and, by the grace of God, the refinance went through. We were now debt-free, except for our mortgage. But the underlying processes that had led us into debt hadn't changed. Chad's business had been failing for a long time, I would later learn. He continued to manage our finances, and a few years later the phone started ringing again.

Then came the default notice. I burned with anger. How could I have been so stupid to let this happen again? I made up my mind. I was not going to stand by passively and lose my home. To complicate matters, my sister and her family were also living in the house we were on the verge of losing. They had moved in when my brother-in-law became ill. By now, Holly had heard me through the vent in her bedroom sobbing many nights. She'd witnessed Chad's rants and his road rage, and her entire family now walked on eggshells as I did. My sister often begged me to go to counseling, but I resisted with the excuse that we didn't have the money.

But eventually Holly was back on her feet and ready to purchase a home. After giving up on finding a house for sale that she liked as much as the one we were all living in, she proposed buying ours. Then Chad and I could buy a different house, and maybe Chad would finally be happy. He seemed energized by the idea of moving. Somehow, as crazy as it sounds, he was able to convince her it would be best for all of us if she bought a house for Chad and me and the boys to move into. I wasn't the only one being controlled by Chad.

Fast forward several years. I'm lying on my bed, staring at another default notice, crying out to God for help.

This marked a turning point. I told Chad I was taking control of our finances. Surprisingly, he gave in fairly easily. I give glory to God for this. My job payed a good hourly wage, and I could work almost unlimited overtime. I secured a second job and worked sixty to eighty hours per week. I was totally exhausted and missed spending time with my kids but was resolved to get us back on track. At first, Chad seemed relieved and supportive. He did the laundry and sometimes rubbed my shoulders. He took care of the kids and made their lunches. He started painting the house and pulled some weeds. I felt an optimism I hadn't known in a long while.

But quickly Chad became moody again. He sat in his office for hours on end, staring at his computer. Dirty dishes piled in the sink and our lawn ran amok. The painting project was abandoned. Broken things stayed broken. The house my sister owned was falling down around me for lack of care. I call this time in my life *the pit*. One day, the neighbors even complained.

"They can go to hell!" Chad shouted.

Although we were slowly digging out, it was apparent that even my two jobs wouldn't sustain us. Barring divine intervention, this pit would swallow me whole.

Again I cried out to God. (Are you noticing a recurring theme?) God was about to answer my plea . . . again.

A Miracle

Chad informed me that he spent so much time in his office because he was desperately looking for work during a terrible economic time, and jobs were scarce. After thirty years of self-employment, he decided that his only option was to become a long-haul truck driver. My initial reaction was "Absolutely not!" There had to be another way, for the kids' sake. Should we sell our home and move out of state? No, that wouldn't work. Our middle schoolers were plugged into a good church, an active Boy Scout troop, and friend group. Truck driving was our only option. Even though every warm feeling for Chad had been stomped out of me by this time, I hated to think of him out on the road alone, away from the kids.

Chad's willingness to perform this sacrificial act was a flat out miracle. After years of the entitlement mindset characteristic of batterers, after all the lies, after allowing me to work two jobs, he was putting our family first. I genuinely felt bad, and I couldn't understand why God hadn't made another away.

But as usual, God knew exactly what he was doing.

Soon after Chad left for trucking school, unexpected changes took place in me. My chronic stomach aches improved. My chest pains resolved. I no longer had dizzy spells. My anxiety and heaviness of heart melted away, and I no longer felt uneasy. Most significantly, my night terrors—which, up to this point, had been assaulting me at least once a week—all but disappeared. These were graphic and painful visions of being brutally murdered or trying to escape from some terrifying situation. Without exception, my nightmares had two recurring themes: I was isolated and alone. And just as I was about to die, I would cry out to Jesus knowing I was soon going to be with him. Sometimes I would awaken to see a dark face staring at me, mere inches from my face. Were these episodes psychological? Was I being tormented by demons? Could it be both?

At first I had difficulty discerning exactly what to call my new state of mind. But finally, I put my finger on it. I was happy. I was lighthearted. I had joy. I wasn't walking on eggshells. I wasn't afraid. Little by little, the scales fell off my eyes.

I realized that how I had been living was . . . *wrong*.

While my life drastically improved with Chad's month-long absences, his drastically deteriorated. Trucking isn't all about freedom and the open road. Trucking can be hellish, even for an emotionally well person. So one can only imagine how the harsh life that came with truck driving affected my husband. When he came home, he was resentful and increasingly dark. "You have no idea what I go through on the road. You can't even imagine the things I have seen." He stomped around the house and made sure everyone knew how miserable his life was.

A few years prior to these events, my sister had suffered the tragic loss of her teenage son in a motorcycle accident. Now, God used Holly to hoist me out of my pit. As she plodded through life after losing her boy, she realized that living where she had raised her baby was just too painful. She asked for my permission to sell the house I was living in. Our family would then move back into the one we still owned. Holly had taken wonderful care of my original house. The house we were living in, however, was run-down, half-painted, and in need of repair. While she and her husband took excellent care of my investment, hers had been falling apart.

They poured thousands of dollars and hard work into my pit to get it ready for market. As I painted alongside them and helped sand the floors, they never made me feel anything but loved. Although it was humbling to have them rescue me again, I was too grateful to them and to God to let my pride keep me stuck. My countless hours pleading with God to save me were being answered. I sensed a fresh start was coming.

But first I had to endure Chad's bitterness. He believed my sister had betrayed us.

Meanwhile, I was at last coming to come to grips with the fact that I did not respect my husband as a man. Not only was I terrified of him, I had zero affection for him. I began being honest with the Lord about my hatred and resentment, and I asked him to free me. For the first time, a year had gone by without any physical intimacy. Prior to that, I'd never refused Chad sexually, thinking it was a disobedience to God. Now that Chad had redeemed himself in a big way by stepping up to the plate and doing a job he hated, I asked the Lord to help me forgive him. And I let Chad know I was open to repairing things between us. Maybe the house change, along with a heart change on my part, would usher in my fresh start.

7

TWENTY SECONDS OF COURAGE

I f I have learned anything, it is that wishing for something doesn't make it so. Despite my willingness to reconnect, Chad became more dark. And this was different. There was an edge to him that bordered on menacing. Something had changed for the worse. He was seething.

Whenever he came into the house, it was as if a dark presence entered with him. Our conversations were tenuous. He often cursed God for what his life had become. He frequently complained that he had experienced things on the road so horrible I couldn't possibly imagine. Once he came home with a mark on his face, saying he had been jumped by two thugs in the middle of the night. He had beaten them both with a steel baton and was sure he sent at least one of them to the hospital. On more than one occasion, he told me beating those thugs was "therapeutic" and he actually enjoyed doing it. Was he sending me a message?

Then we had a life-altering conversation. We were discussing a friend who was in the middle of a separation initiated by his wife. The man was worried she was hiding another relationship. Chad looked intensely at me. "If you ever have an affair with another man, I will kill you both," he said. We were in a public setting, and at first I let it go. I was used to him spewing venomous statements. But later that evening while I was painting the bathroom, my entire body became covered with goosebumps. I felt an intense foreboding, and his "I will kill you both" declaration came to the forefront of my mind. I put down my paintbrush and sat still. *What is it going to take?* I heard the Spirit whisper. A danger warning.

I took a deep breath and walked into the room where Chad was sitting. "I need to talk with you about something you said earlier." He glared at me. "Earlier you said you would kill me if I ever had an affair. I am the mother of your children. No matter what you did to me, I would never kill you, because it would devastate our kids. Could you really kill me?" I held my breath.

Chad considered it for a while and then looked directly into my eyes. "Okay," he said, as if he was offering a mercy I didn't deserve, "I will just maim you, and I will kill the guy."

I walked away. The darkness and hatred in Chad's eyes had told the truth. Affair or no, my husband was capable of maiming and killing me. Without remorse. A heaviness fell on me as I returned to my painting. The inner voice spoke again. *This is going to happen. It doesn't have to. Run to me.*

I Want to Live

God had miraculously plucked me out of my impossible pit—from mounds of debt and a house I couldn't take care of—and placed me in a home that was not in need of repair. Furthermore, Chad's meager income, to the penny, allowed us to pay our bills. But his increasing darkness, combined with the blinders falling off my vision, led to a prison of fear. My despair was more intense than ever. Here's why. For the first time in years, I did not have a desire to die.

I wanted to live! I had two beautiful kids who needed me, and I wasn't ready to suffer a violent death. Yet I knew . . . I was *going* to die, and there was nothing anyone could do about it.

I expressed my concerns to my sister. "I guess I'm going to end up in a ditch somewhere, and I just have to accept it." Holly agreed about the danger yet felt powerless to stop it. She had seen what Chad was capable of, and she too was despairing. So affected by my abuse was she that she couldn't step back and see that my thinking was completely darkened. We cried.

I felt it was my responsibility to prepare for my untimely death. I increased my life insurance. I made a will. I stopped eating, and I couldn't sleep. But I also prayed.

And I felt strongly that God was giving me Romans 12:12 as my key verse for this time. "Be joyful in hope, patient in affliction, faithful in prayer." *Lord, you know I have been patient in affliction, and I have been asking you in prayer to heal Chad for over twenty years. But how can I be joyful in hope?*

Even though the Lord didn't answer me directly, he impressed upon my heart that this was his message for me. Meanwhile, Holly moved across the country. No one else knew what I was going through. I would often be in my pajamas by six o'clock in the evening, lying in bed, feeling isolated, staring at the ceiling, and wondering why my life had turned out this way.

As usual, while I lay paralyzed with fear, God was working behind the scenes, setting the stage for his amazing work in me. I met a woman named Steph who had kids my age and who shared my love for surfing. Although she knew nothing about what I was going through, she gave me a book detailing how God intervened in one woman's life of abuse. The book was an easy read, and something struck me. Throughout her life, the author had a group of friends who lived through everything with her, and she with them. There were no secrets between them. She called this group of friends her "dolphin pod."

I needed a pod. Although I had many casual friends, and one or two that were fairly close, I hadn't let anyone in on my private struggles.

At this same time, a neighbor and lifelong friend was going through a trial of epic proportions. Her husband was perpetrating such evil on her and her children that life as she knew it was blown to pieces. One of the most Spirit-filled followers of Jesus I had ever met, she literally radiated with the power of the Christ, even while facing a trial that would have sent most to the psychiatric ward. I went to visit her.

Although she was in major trauma herself, she asked how I was doing. "I'm worried about you."

Her genuine concern took me off guard, and I found myself leaking tidbits of top secret information. "Chad has an anger problem, and it's getting difficult to deal with."

She listened quietly while I confessed some highly guarded truths. Including the death threat.

"So when are you going to get a divorce?"

I was shocked. "I can't get a divorce!"

"Why not?" she asked in all innocence, then waited patiently while I tried my best to formulate a reply.

"Because I'm a Christian."

She looked confused. "But you're being abused and your life is in danger."

I couldn't disagree. "Yes, but I would rather die than get a divorce."

I walked away from that conversation scratching my head and wondering why I preferred death over divorce. And a few days later, as I spent more and more time praying and in my Bible, I felt the Spirit urging me to finally take my sister's advice and get help.

I once heard a sermon based on the premise that twenty seconds of courage can change your life. My twenty seconds of courage came when I called the Employee Assistance Program through my work to ask if counseling was available and determine the cost.

"EAP, my name is Christine. How may I help you today?" I nearly hung up. She seemed to sense my hesitance. "We are here to help. What can I do for you?"

When I explained that I needed counseling, Christine asked questions, some of which I wasn't ready to answer truthfully (Was I in danger?). So I didn't. She authorized the sessions and even gave me a list of counselors who identified themselves as Christians. Much to my surprise, I discovered that the first five sessions were free. After that, there would be only a forty-dollar co-pay for unlimited sessions. My palms were covered with sweat when I hung up. I moved on to courageous step number two.

The Spirit had been prompting me to call a specific friend, Michelle—a servant-hearted prayer warrior for Jesus. She had often freaked me out with how Spirit-filled she was, as I wasn't brought up in a charismatic tradition. But I knew she was a rock solid Christian. I shook as I dialed her number and secretly hoped she wouldn't answer. Would she believe me? Would she think badly of me?

Yet God gave me the courage to tell her the truth about what was happening in my home and to ask for her help. She said I must come to her house that night for prayer and that I absolutely needed to meet with her pastor.

Later that afternoon, I prayed for wisdom and asked God to lead me to the right counselor. I called the one whose office was closest to my home. My appointment was the following day. As I hung up, I realized that when I finally decided to seek help, God had provided for me instantly. He was watching. He was waiting. And he was able to help.

A New Creation

Therefore, if anyone is in Christ, the new creation has come. The old has gone, the new is here!

2 Corinthians 5:17

lthough I had read this verse hundreds, possibly even thousands, of times, and while I believed it to be true, I didn't realize God could transform *me* in *one night*. But that is exactly what he did.

When I arrived at Michelle's house for prayer, I was burdened, trembling, and hopeless. By now, Chad seemed able to rationalize behaviors that would have previously generated a tearful apology. Several times over the years I told Chad that if he refused to change, he was going to lose me. To which, he confidently proclaimed that I did not have biblical grounds for divorce. It would "destroy my Christian witness." It would "ruin any chance our children had of ever finding love." He had me convinced I wasn't allowed to go anywhere.

Pastor Blaine and I retreated to Michelle's garage, and he sat in horror as I tearfully told him everything I'd been through, and of the Spirit's warning when Chad threatened to kill me. I waited for him to tell me what to do. Instead, he said the words I believe Jesus himself, if sitting across from me in that garage, would have used. "Jenny," he spoke thoughtfully, "God don't make no junk. You aren't junk, you got me?" I stared at him and shook my head. "God never intended for you to be abused, and you need to get that guy out of there for your safety. Then you can try to save the marriage, if there is anything to save. But safety comes first. You don't gotta die."

I pondered his words. "But won't that blow my Christian witness?" His response changed my life. "So what?" he said calmly. "That is why Christ died."

I felt like I got slapped in the face, in a good way. A *snap out of it!* way. The kind of slap you use to revive someone who was drowning in the ocean. All my life I'd been striving to earn God's love and favor. And now, in an instant I discerned the reason I'd chosen death over divorce. I was afraid God would forsake me if I left.

The truth was, if Chad had committed adultery, I would have leapt for joy—and left. If he had hurt our sons, I'd have gone without looking back. But with the exception of an occasional reckless-driving incident, he had reserved his anger for me. Why had it been so difficult for me to see that his abuse toward me was vile sin in the eyes of God? But now I was walking in the truth: I was living in abuse.

After praying for me, Pastor Blaine left me in the good hands of Michelle and her friends. These beautiful, amazing women of God spent three hours listening to my story and weeping, laying hands on me, and anointing me with oil. That night, I was truly healed. Michelle received specific words from the Spirit and led me in prayer, in her sweet way. "Can you say, 'Jesus, I give you fear.'"

I repeated after her. "Jesus, I give you fear."

Then, "Jesus, I give you shame."

"Jesus, I give you disappointment."

"Jesus, I give you lost dreams."

"Jesus, I give you terror."

"Jesus, I give you secrecy."

"Jesus, I give you isolation."

"Jesus, I give you hopelessness."

I released these burdens to my Jesus, and he took them all. Not figuratively, but literally. "I choose to forgive Chad, in Jesus' name. I choose to refuse to participate in the cover-up, in Jesus' name. I renounce my covenant with fear, in Jesus' name. I release the fear of being murdered, in Jesus' name. I release the fear of losing my children, in Jesus' name. I release the fear of being abandoned by God, in Jesus' name."

Without a doubt, this was the most transformative work God ever performed in my life. One of the women prayed I would hunger and thirst for God's Word, and she equipped me with Psalm 91 and Isaiah 61 as a start. When the night ended, I truly felt like a new creation.

Everyone said I was radiant, and that my countenance had completely changed.

For the first time in a very long while, I had hope. I had been patient in affliction, I had been faithful in prayer, and now I was joyful in hope. And all in one night, I had found my dolphin pod! Nothing had changed in my physical situation, but everything had changed in my spiritual condition.

Journal entry:

Jesus says that when we know the truth it sets us free, and Jesus is right. Suddenly I am no longer totally focused and consumed with my husband, our relationship, how to fix him, how to stop his abuse, or how to change in order to make him better. Now my focus is where it should have been all along—on the freedom, safety, health, happiness, & well-being of myself and my children. I am not sure exactly how to get there but I have an ace in the hole. The almighty God who spoke the world into existence and has walked with me the entire time loves me and my kids. He hates violence and he will protect me and give me the tools to stay safe. He is with me, and if Chad decides to "show me what a monster looks like," I will call upon the Name of the Lord and he will show Chad what real power looks like.

Discernment and Direction

I will repay you for the years the locusts have eaten. . . . and you will praise the name of the Lord your God, who has worked wonders for you; never again will my people be shamed.

Joel 2:25–26

I spent the next several months earnestly seeking God and asking for his guidance. One of the many evidences that his Spirit was leading me on this journey was the fact that my counselor was a Bible-believing woman of God. Up until the time I shared my secret with my prayer pod and began hashing through many difficult sessions with my counselor, I had only spoken of Chad's behaviors using terms like *mental illness, anger problems, out of control, mean,* and *crazy.* I hadn't been ready to face the truth that I was being abused. My counselor handed me a paper listing several categories of abuse—physical, emotional, verbal, sexual, and financial. Listed under each category were a number of specific behaviors. Had I been subjected to anything on the list? she asked. My heart sank.

"All but two."

In Michelle's garage, we prayed weekly for Chad's deliverance and my safety. They prophesied rescue over me, declaring that God was going to restore "what the locusts had eaten" and grant me a double portion for my shame. They anointed every door and window in my home with oil, and together we rebuked the spirit of violence and abuse. We prayed God would command his angels concerning me and protect me.

My new church was Spirit-filled and totally different than anything I had ever experienced. Each time I went to a service, it seemed the pastor confirmed exactly what God had revealed to me in our time together earlier in the week. It felt as if God was doing open-heart surgery on me without anesthesia. Only a few months earlier, I was not even attending church regularly, and now I couldn't survive without constant fellowship. I went to church every Sunday and Wednesday and wept like a child before my *Abba,* my heavenly Father. And I prayed like never before, flat on my face, tears staining my cheeks. I devoured the Word of God and felt I would drown without it. I listened to nothing but worship music and sobbed through the songs.

This wasn't like those "mountaintop" experiences I'd had following a youth retreat or an in-depth Bible study, during which I got fired up and made all kinds of promises to God. This was the exact opposite. I was not on the mountaintop. I was walking through the valley of the shadow of death, facing the depths of my darkness. Any silly notion I held about being good enough for God was swept away. I moved from *I should pray, I should read the Word, I should sing praises, I should fellowship,* to having a deep desire to simply be in the presence of the living God. And there he was. Jesus. Sitting there at my kitchen table, or on the edge of my bed whenever I needed to talk with him. Just as he always had been. He didn't say, "I told you so." He just ministered to me. He listened as I poured out my disappointments. He didn't become irritated when I complained that all I ever wanted was a loving marriage or asked him how he'd let such things happen when I had done "everything right." He just loved me.

Through it all, I was trying to discern whether or not to seek a divorce. The Spirit revealed in many ways that on my current course, I would die at the hands of my husband. Living in the power of the Spirit, I was finally able to conclude that a mom in the grave was not a good option for my kids. That was *Satan's* best-case scenario, and I was no longer going to lay down without a fight! First Peter 5:8 describes the devil as an enemy who "prowls around like a roaring lion looking for someone to devour," and he had been having a free-for-all with me for too long. But I was starting to understand spiritual warfare and my eyes were now open to his workings.

Many times I asked God why he did not answer my prayers for Chad's healing. I discerned through this time of wrestling with my Redeemer that he'd heard every single word I uttered and tear I'd cried. The abuse continued for one simple reason: Chad rejected God's discipline and refused to repent. Abuse is sin, and willful disobedience to God leads to a hardened heart. God wanted to heal Chad. But Chad's choices were wreaking havoc on all of our lives.

During this time, I was very open with Chad and explained my new understanding. This, as you can imagine, did not go over well! He insisted we both had things to work on, not just him. He assured me that if I found a counselor for us to go to together, he would do whatever it took to save the marriage. So I called my Employee Assistance Program again and asked for a Christian counselor who was male. I was worried about two women in a room alone with Chad if he became enraged. Perhaps a man would provide more protection. The counselor I chose suggested we meet ahead of time to discuss my concerns. Chad could join us at the next session.

I launched into my saga. Not two minutes in—I hadn't even gotten to the "lowlights" yet—he stopped me. "You need to read a book called *The Battered Woman* by Lenore Walker," he said, then urged me to continue.[1]

That's odd. I haven't even told him anything yet. I proceeded to tell how I got where I was and ended with, "I'm thinking of seeking a divorce, and my husband asked that we go to counseling first." It was already clear to me that I could not stay married unless Chad had a radical, miraculous transformation. Otherwise, I would end the marriage.

Once again, the Spirit had led me to exactly the right counselor. "Even if only thirty percent of what you are saying is true," he said, adding that he believed every word, "any Catholic priest would annul your marriage right now. Having said that, if there is any hope of saving your marriage, things need to change immediately."

And then he told me all the ways I was culpable. Keeping silent had perpetuated the abuse. Chad was the devil's biggest fool, but I needed to stop enabling his behavior. What's more, Chad needed to face up to the reality of his sin, and there needed to be actual consequences. It was going to take serious work, but with God, and with Chad's willing participation, there was hope. Chad would have to agree to attend weekly support groups for men who batter, and groups for adults of childhood dysfunction. And the next time I felt threatened, I had to call the police so there were consequences.

He also advised me to seek a legal separation and tell Chad to move out while he attended his groups and worked on his changes. I should set a timeline of at least six months before I would consider reconciliation. I expressed my concern that Chad was highly suspicious and had already been interrogating me about whether I "had someone else." The counselor's answer was so amazing I wrote it down word for word.

"You tell him," he said with conviction, "I am not going to fulfill any of your evil fantasies by seeking another relationship." Man, this guy was good. When he told me to cling to Christ while Chad and I were temporarily apart, I knew he was giving me godly advice. But did I have the strength to do what was needed? Most likely not. But thankfully, God's power is made strong in our weaknesses (2 Corinthians 12:9).

I could depend on him to help me do the impossible.

9

PREPARING FOR BATTLE

I fired up the computer and browsed Amazon's preview pages of the book the counselor had recommended. Another book caught my eye, *Why Does He do That? Inside the Minds of Angry and Controlling Men* by Lundy Bancroft. I had asked that very question so many times! So I downloaded that one first. I put the kids in bed and started reading at 10:30 at night, noting the author's warning that the information could be "difficult because it awakens feelings and realizations that are overwhelming."[1] Three hours in, I was dry heaving in the bathroom. And hyperventilating.

Reading what was virtually my own biography was one of the most gut-wrenching experiences of my life. I turned each page, whispering, "no . . . no . . . no," trembling a little more with each chapter.

The author deftly showed how every excuse I had ever given Chad for his behavior was actually a "myth" of abuse, and he dismantled the illogical thinking behind each and every one. The bottom line was . . . everything I endured was purposeful. "It was all on purpose!" I wailed at the top of my lungs. "Twenty-two years, wasted! I gave you the best years of my life!"

I was both horrified and liberated. Everything rang true, and the book was filled with actual quotes from abusers and the women who had been victimized. I had heard Chad utter the same exact words. And I'd said exactly what the other victims had said. The book gave me a new awareness and the ability to respond appropriately to the manipulations that come with abuse. Although a painful step in my journey, I knew God had led me to it.

Shortly thereafter, Chad came home for a week. I was folding laundry in the bedroom when he approached me. "I just wanted to let you know that I called Focus on the Family," he said. "I told them a little about what's going on in our marriage because I wanted to get some godly advice. I've also been in touch with Ron." Ron was a counselor Chad and I had seen on a few occasions at one time. "I told him I don't exactly know what's going on with you, but I thought one of the reasons you're so upset is that I said I was going to kill you. Or at least maim you." He said this as if it was casual, loving banter. "Anyway, I was wrong to say that."

Now the old me would have thought, *Oh good, he called Focus on the Family so everything is going to be fine.* I'd have embraced denial like an old friend. But I was a new creation now. I was walking in the truth, painful as it was. From now on I was going to respond in the truth. And not with rage. Christ had traded my rage for quiet strength. I wasn't even tempted to scream in anger. Christ had freed me from that too. Instead, I began to question him, specifically about his conversation with Ron. I asked how the counselor responded to his confession. "Ron said it was wrong to say something like that to you, and he's right. I am sorry."

I told him, without raising my voice, that a glib apology wasn't going to make up for twenty-two years of terror. And that I doubted the sincerity of his apology. And that I didn't accept it. I was firm. I was calm. And I was determined to relate to him in a new way, in the power of the Spirit.

My response threw him off. "I did not come in here and apologize just to get your hostility!" he hissed.

"You don't deserve anything more than that," I said, returning my attention to the laundry. He stormed out.

Journal entry:

I'm walking in a new-found strength, and I just had an epiphany. Chad actually told someone he has threatened to kill me. I wonder how it will look when Ron hears the rest of the story. In a battle of wits—me versus Chad—I will lose. So I asked God to go to battle for me and specifically to cause Chad to make a misstep. Answered prayer number—too many to count! I love you, Father! Lead me and keep me safe, in your holy name.

A few days later I went to see Ron with the purpose of telling him that if I ended up in a ditch somewhere, went missing, or was killed in some "accidental way," it would be his moral duty to go to the police with Chad's confession. Statistically speaking, battered women are at the highest risk of being killed while pregnant and when trying to leave the relationship. Chad was highly intelligent, and I didn't want him getting away with my murder.

Ron, this sweet, elderly saint, looked like he was trying to hold back tears as I told him the truth of my situation. He sighed and looked sorrowful and asked me a question that would be repeated by many in the months to come. "Why didn't you tell me this sooner?"

I told him that mostly I was too ashamed and scared to say anything. He looked genuinely sad. "What would you like me to do for you?" I launched into the reason for my visit.

Ron's response stunned me. "He said no such thing."

My head was spinning. It never occurred to me Chad had lied. The entire conversation was a fabrication and the implications were chilling. It had been an attempt to manipulate me into staying. If he could lie so convincingly about this, what else was he lying about?

I left perplexed. In prayer, I brought the issue before the Lord. How and when should I bring up the issue of separation? Very clearly the Spirit assured me not to worry. When the time came, I'd know.

Shadows Before Shelter

While these events were unfolding, I was making plans for a safe escape should violence erupt. From a local women's shelter, I received instructions on how to pack a "safety bag" that I could grab and run out of the house with in case I was attacked. It contained a change of clothes for me and the boys, copies of important documents, toiletries, and cash. I kept the number of the shelter, my cell phone, and my car keys on me at all times.

While Chad was away, I collected the guns he had stored in our house and garage and locked them in a closet. Then I piled a mess of things in front of the closet door. With the help of my counselor, I gathered my courage to tell a few key people about my situation. I confided in my friend Steph and one of my neighbors. I told my manager, so that if I didn't arrive at work or check in, she would be alerted and notify police. Often the Spirit would place someone on my heart and say, *Tell them.* I was leery at first, but quickly learned that listening to him and obeying his prompting always turned out for my good. On more than one occasion, the Spirit even informed the person ahead of time. They already knew what I was going to say. This confirmation gave me even greater courage. And people did not think badly of me! Rather, they were genuinely sad and concerned. All my fears of being rejected and looked down on had been completely unfounded.

Throughout this time my prayer was, "Heavenly Father, you know my heart. I want to do your will. Please lead me." Jesus says if we ask anything in his name in accordance with God's will, it will be given to us (Matthew 7:7–11). I was asking him to lead me, and he was in the business of answering prayer.

Yet God was about to lead me down a path so dark that if he had given me a glimpse of what was to come, I would have turned back.

10

THE RECKONING

Journal entry:

Life is about to get scary because Chad is coming home for the next four days. Sleep is always difficult for me when he is here, so I am trusting in God to allow me to sleep in peace and protect me from nightmares. I also need to walk in the Spirit to avoid responding in the flesh, allowing hostility or rage to surface. I surrendered my rights to anger, bitterness, malice, and resentment at the foot of the Cross in my prayer time this morning, and that is where they need to stay. Thank you heavenly Father for your mercy, guidance, and protection. I love you so much.

Chad did in fact come home, the very next day. Perhaps prophetically, life was indeed about to get scary.

Upon his arrival, things were tense but we played nice because we had my son's birthday party to get through. Chad was on edge the next day, making multiple comments about how his job was not secure, while I sat at the kitchen table paying bills. "I might as well just get let it go and collect unemployment and stay home from now on," he said.

I looked up from the bills. "We need your income."

Chad glared. "Thanks for telling me that. I had no idea!" he said, through gritted teeth. "You know what? Why don't you just serve me divorce papers?"

I remembered the Spirit's assurance that the right moment to bring up the issue of separation would present itself, and here it was. I was filled with a strange calm. "All right. I will."

His face beet red, Chad leaned over me. "Excuse me? What did you say?"

"I said I will. I cannot continue to live like this, and you refuse to change your behavior, so I will serve you papers."

Chad's next words in a weird way showed that he knew, deep down, what he had done. "I have never abused you even once!" Then, as if another being took over his body, he yanked out his cell phone and shoved it into my face. "Guess what?" he hissed. "I've been secretly recording our phone conversations for months! I have one of your own voice saying that I never hit you." My mind flashed back to an odd conversation of a month earlier, when Chad had demanded I answer him. "I just want to get something straight. I never hit you, right?" he had said. Everything was becoming clear.

Now wearing a sinister grin, he pressed his face against mine. "I'm never going back on the road. I am going to stay right here and I am going to watch your every move. You are never, never going to be allowed to be alone with our sons. I'm going to install security cameras all over this house and watch you twenty-four hours a day." The darkness in his eyes told the truth—he wanted me dead. I grasped the kitchen counter so I wouldn't faint with terror.

Chad ran upstairs and flung my son's bedroom door open. "Your mom has something to tell you! Go ahead, Mom, tell your son about your plan, you lying . . . " I couldn't believe the vile words coming out of his mouth in front of our son.

"I am so sorry, honey. This has nothing to do with you." Seth looked confused and terrified. I ran downstairs. Chad followed, pressing against me. I could feel his hot breath against the back of my neck. "Please leave me alone!" I ran into my bedroom and tried to close the door. Chad kicked it open. He folded his arms across his chest and spread his feet wide, blocking the door with his body.

"Get away from me!" He wouldn't budge. I was trapped. But when he pressed into me again, trying to force me farther into the bedroom, I bolted around him and ran toward the kitchen. I grabbed the phone with my trembling hands.

"If you are ever scared, call the police," I had been advised. My heart raced as I dialed 9-1-1.

"What is your emergency?"

"Please help me. My husband is angry, following me around the house. He's intimidating me, and I'm so frightened!"

"Does your husband have any weapons?"

"Yes! But they're all locked in a closet."

"A unit is on the way."

Chad called Seth downstairs and made him sit at the table. "Your mother is trying to get me thrown in jail! What do you think about that?"

Fear washed over my son's face. "Mom, why?" Just then, two officers arrived, one tall and blonde, the other stocky and dark. They sent my confused son upstairs and then separated Chad and me. Next I got a lecture. "Look ma'am, we're cops, okay? We don't like these kinds of calls. This is for the courts. Even if we took your husband to jail, he would be right back out tomorrow. You need to find another way to handle this."

I couldn't believe my ears. Weren't the police supposed to help? They told Chad to be nice and left me with the monster. Chad grabbed me by the arm, marched me upstairs and commanded me to sit on a chair in my son's room. Seth looked bewildered and frightened. Chad pulled out his cell phone again. "Your mom is a bold-faced liar, son! She keeps changing her story and it's time for her to stop lying. Now it's time for me to record your lies!" He pushed the record button and shoved his phone in my face.

Watching the pain in my son's face, I wanted to die. "I am so sorry. I have nothing to say, and I don't want your dad recording me."

"That's because you're a bold-faced liar!" Chad yelled, then called me a name.

"I am not a liar."

"Why do you keep changing your story then? Why did you call the cops, huh? To get me thrown in jail!"

My son was crying, pleading with me to let his dad record me. "If you don't want him to record you, it must be because you're lying, Mom. Just do the right thing and tell the truth." I was devastated.

Things deteriorated further when Micah got home. Soon Chad had both of my beautiful children turned against me. And the torture went on late into the night. Chad paced like an animal, screaming obscenities at me between fits of crying. "Why is she doing this to us?" he would say. "Your mother doesn't love you. I will do anything to save the marriage, but she won't!"

"Boys," I would attempt to reason. "It's not right for your dad to call me those names."

But they just sobbed and continued to defend their father. "He's only doing it because you are breaking his heart."

Finally, the boys went to bed—furious with me. Chad planted himself on the couch, which was right next to my escape route—the garage door. I closed the bedroom door, turned the lock, and dialed the shelter. "I don't know what to do," I whispered to the hotline volunteer. "I think I'm going to be killed tonight."

"You need to get out of there now."

"I can't get past my husband."

"Can you call the police?" I explained why that wouldn't work. Finally I promised her I would call again if I was physically attacked, and hung up. I did not sleep through that long, hellish night. Just sat up in bed, wondering how it was going to happen. Would he strangle me with the hair-dryer cord? Suffocate me with a pillow? Was he going to shoot me?

I prayed and wept and waited for daylight.

Get out now. I heard the voice of the Spirit warning me repeatedly, as morning dawned and things started right back up. Chad was seething.

Fortunately, he was forced to leave the house briefly, and I decided to make my escape. I tore upstairs and woke up my teenage son. "I know you don't understand, honey, but we are not safe here. We need to go to a shelter. Now." Seth looked conflicted, but said he didn't want me to go and he wouldn't be coming with me if I did go. I bolted downstairs and tried to convince Micah we needed to leave. He and I were inseparable. He was my snuggle buddy.

He thought about it. "But Dad is going to be mad."

I stroked his hair. "Dad won't know. We will be in a shelter and we will be safe. Please, we need to go now!"

Micah looked torn. "Is Seth coming?"

"No honey, he doesn't want to come."

"Then I don't want to come either."

And then my moment passed. Chad returned and he started calling me ugly names again. I knew that if I loved my sons, I needed to leave. They could not be exposed to this any longer. So I grabbed my safety bag in one hand and held onto Christ with the other. I got in my car and drove away.

It was Mother's Day.

Shelter

Numbness set in as I phoned the shelter. Then tears, explaining that my sons would not come with me.

The tender voice on the line reassured me. "We know that 75 percent of children will side with the abuser. But what is most important now is your safety. Your kids will come around in time." She gave me directions to what she called a "safety net"—a motel in a secret location. I was to check in under an assumed name and wait for a phone call from a shelter representative the following morning.

First, I needed to stock up on some food and make any necessary phone calls because I would not be allowed to use the phone once I entered the safe house. One of the calls I made was to my friend Michelle.

"Jenny," she spoke calmly and firmly, "this morning I had a vision of God plucking you out of that home. Your sons are going to be fine.

God showed me that he needed to remove you alone. You are going to be okay. We'll pray for you." Later I learned that my beautiful pod got together for their usual morning surf, then instead prayed for me.

I pulled into the safe house exhausted and starving and bewildered. When I gave the attendant my assumed name, she looked at me knowingly and handed me a key. As I shut the door behind me and peered around that dark little room, the reality of my situation hit me like a Mack Truck. I fell to the ground.

> *Journal entry:*
>
> *This isn't what rescue looks like. I misspoke when I wrote that yesterday was the worst day of my life. Today is Mother's Day. And while others are out being celebrated and loved on, I am sitting in a motel room alone, waiting to hear if I will be accepted into a shelter. And my sons believe that I am a liar, selfish, and that I am breaking up the family. No, this is by far the worst day of my life.*
>
> *I have been praying, fasting, seeking wise council, and clinging to your promises. You promise to "make the righteousness of my cause shine like the noonday sun" (Psalm 37:6) and "not to harm but for a hope and a future" (Jeremiah 29:11). You said that because I love you and call on your name you will rescue me (Psalm 91:14). But as I sit here alone I don't see any of these being fulfilled. I see my enemy prospering, spending a cozy night with my beautiful sons, who are being filled with lies from Satan right now. So Lord, if you are real, you need to act. I want to believe your words, but I am in a serious crisis of doubt right now. Please reveal yourself to me in this most desperate moment of my life.*

Hour after hour, lying in the fetal position, hugging tight my son's clothing, I heard nothing from the Spirit. Silence. Darkness. Despair. By late afternoon, I'd reached my breaking point. *Jesus, do you even exist? I am going to turn on my phone, and I want there to be a message from you. Something that tells me you are real. Or it is over between us.*

At 4:32 p.m., I switched on my phone and watched as it completed its startup. At 4:33, a text message came in from a friend. Just one word. "Jesus."

I stared at the name. And then I made a decision. *Okay, Lord. I have nothing. But I am going to praise you. I choose to believe.*

And I starting singing.

Through sobs, I sang the only lyrics that would come to me, a modern praise song based on Psalm 121:1–2, "I lift my eyes up to the mountains—where does my help come from? My help comes from the LORD, the Maker of heaven and earth."

"Oh how I need you Lord . . . . Come and give me light," I sang."[1]

My voice became strong and clear as I repeated this song over and over. I felt the power of the Holy Spirit and raised my arms to the sky proclaiming the goodness of God. "Oh God, you are faithful and true! There is none like you! You are exalted above the earth and I will trust in you because you are my deliverer! Holy, holy, holy is the Lord God Almighty! Let the weak say I am strong because of what the Lord has done!"

There I was, underweight, exhausted, and beaten down, but proclaiming the wonders and promises of God. Suddenly I looked above me and saw of vision of heaven. A multitude of people in white robes, cheering for me. Clapping and pumping their fists in the air. Shouting for joy. At the front was my nephew Michael, who had tragically been killed as a teenager a few years prior, looking exactly as I remembered. His dark brown skin stood out in striking contrast against the white of his robe. And I saw my brother, David, who was only thirty-six when God took him. But he looked different. On earth he had been severely autistic and had a seizure disorder. He was balding and skinny, and as a result of all his medication, his face had changed, his complexion became sallow, and his teeth needed work. But now he had beautiful skin tone, straight, white teeth, an entire mop of loose brown-blonde curls. And I saw my friend's daughter Heather, who had been overtaken by cancer and went to heaven at the tender age of twenty-six. She too did not look anything like I remembered her—now healthy and smiling beautifully.

And there were a multitude of others watching and cheering as I literally beat back the Devil by the power of the Holy Spirit. The vision was gone after a few seconds, and I said, "Lord, you say you will command your angels concerning me, and I want to see that." Later I wrote about my amazing experience.

Journal entry:

Jesus is here. He is weeping with me. He is wiping my tears. He is shielding the hearts and minds of my sons from the attacks of the evil one. He is wiping their tears and he wants to wipe away Chad's tears.

I started singing praise songs. It sounded like a cow giving birth at first because of all the sobbing but before long my voice was strong . . . . I am sure I looked like a complete lunatic. For a solid thirty minutes the Spirit came upon me so profoundly I had goose bumps, and I could literally feel the angels in the room. Not just one. A cloud of witnesses . . . . And I realized if I had my sons I would be clinging to them for comfort. If I could call my sister or my friends for support I would be clinging to them instead of Christ. No—it was purposed that my sons not join me here even though it is gut-wrenchingly painful. And I passed the test. In my darkest hour, when I did not feel his presence and I found myself doubting, I cried out and he answered. I believe when I have weathered this storm I will be a "planting of the Lord for the display of his splendor"(Isaiah 61:3). And I will help other women. And it won't be because I was smart or steady or cunning or strong. It will be because Jesus Christ is alive, and the same power that God exerted in raising him from the dead is living in me. He is releasing me from captivity and leading me out of the darkness. That will be my message. Jesus is real, and he does what he says he came to do. Amen!

Michelle's vision had been true. God needed to get me alone so we could settle some things between us. Ephesians 6:12 says, "For our struggle is not against flesh and blood, but against the rulers, against the authorities, against the powers of this dark world and against the spiritual forces of evil in the heavenly realms."

The battle to come was going to be difficult. But now I knew the power behind me, and I knew God would be with me. I pulled back the covers, climbed in bed with a nutrition bar, and turned on the television. A preacher I had never heard of was giving a sermon titled, "Facing Your Mountains."

Using an illustration from the story *Roots*, he told of Kunta Kinte, the slave who had neither freedom nor hope. He suffered horrible humiliation, beatings, and chains. When his wife bore him a daughter, he carried his newborn outside, lifted her to the sky and said, "Behold One who is greater than you."[1] The message was this: Even in the midst of horrible circumstances, we can have hope if we always remember that there is One who is greater, helping us face our mountains.

I smiled for the first time in a while, knowing the preacher's words were meant to reach my ears. I took a few bites, closed my eyes, and prayed God would grant me sleep, then show me what to do next.

11

A New Dawn

By now I hope you've flipped to the back of the book and read "How to Recognize an Abusive Relationship." There we look at the emotional, psychological, and behavioral patterns that are common to abusive relationships. But I need to stress here that the details of each woman's journey *out* of abuse are unique. The decisions I felt led to make, for better or worse, won't necessarily look the same as yours. That's why faith is so, so important. We each need to learn to discern God's voice and follow him with courage every step of the way.

At the end of my path out of darkness would be immense light and victory. But often it felt hidden along the journey. I believe the Lord only gave me enough light for the step in front of me so he could grow my trust. And because I had so much learning to do.

By now God had revealed that I was in a spiritual battle. And if there is anything I want to impress upon you, dear reader, it is that this battle is real. It's not a metaphor. This kind of language might be new to you, as it was for me. But it comes right out of what you might call our "handbook of spiritual warfare," the Holy Bible. "For our struggle is not against flesh and blood, but against the rulers, against the authorities, against the powers of this dark world and against the spiritual forces of evil in the heavenly realms" (Ephesians 6:12). In another passage we read, "For though we live in the world, we do not wage war as the world does. The weapons we fight with are not weapons of the world. On the contrary, they have divine power to demolish strongholds" (2 Corinthians 10:3–4).

Learning how to engage in this kind of warfare proved to be the single most important discovery I had to make on my journey out of the darkness.

Although I realized I was in danger, I could not bear the thought of checking into the shelter without my kids. During the long night, the Lord had given me a plan, and in the morning he gave me the strength I needed to execute it. The shelter volunteers were understandably concerned about the situation to which I was returning. I promised that even though the police had been more harm than help, I would call them again if I were in danger.

My sons messaged me, asking when I was coming home. I let them know I was on my way home and I would be waiting for them after school. "I love you Mom and I can't wait to see you."

Chad was texting me also. And true to form, acting as if nothing had happened. "Hey," he wrote, "Got a big answer to prayer today. I got a local job and I will be staying home from now on. I am glad you are coming home." No apology. No remorse. He told me he had met with a man named Rich and that it was very helpful. Neither of us knew him very well, only that he was a recovered addict who was on fire for Christ and had dedicated his life to helping others.

Unbeknownst to me, the police had been at my house while I was gone. And after being called out two days in a row, they were taking things a little more seriously. Chad had gotten a hold of my cell phone earlier in the week and had read a text message from my neighbor giving me the phone number of an attorney named Leslie who specialized in domestic violence. While I was away, he confronted my neighbor about it and scared the daylights out of her. She called the police. I live in suburbia, and the police don't usually show up at a house two days in a row. So now the neighbors were talking and becoming aware of the situation I had tried so hard for so long to hide.

That morning I went to see Leslie and told her about my night in the shelter. When I recounted my vision, tears rolled down her cheeks. I knew she was exactly the right person to help me. Together we crafted a motion to present to Chad and then to the courts to make it legally enforceable. I would agree to two months of marriage counseling, during which time I would move out of the home 50 percent of the time, and Chad would move out of the home 50 percent of the time. The boys would be able to stay in their home while Chad and I rotated in and out. The boys would be protected from being exposed to their dad's volatility, and I would be safe from risk for a violent attack.

With God all things are possible. So if Chad was willing to do the work necessary to be completely transformed by the Holy Spirit, God could still save the marriage. I was even willing to move out of my home for a week at a time in order to allow this process to take place in safety. Any member of my pod would gladly accept me into their homes, so this seemed a wise plan given to me by the Spirit.

Chad agreed that having Rich mediate was a great idea. I alerted the pod and asked them to pray at three o'clock. We gathered at the kitchen table— Chad, my children, Rich, another longtime friend of ours named Barb, and me. Rich opened us in prayer. Chad wore a look of tender concern on his face as we began. Rich first asked the boys if they had anything to say. "I am sorry that I sent you those mean text messages," Seth said. "I didn't mean what I wrote and I was just really angry. Can you please forgive me?"

I squeezed his hand. "I forgive you."

My younger son said he was afraid I had felt betrayed when he would not come to the shelter with me. I reassured both of my sons that they always and forever had my love, and that nothing they had done could ever change that. Rich told the boys that no matter what was happening, they had two parents who loved them very much.

Then I began, looking directly at my two sons. "I realize that when I called the police it looked like I was trying to put your dad in jail and take you away from him. But I called them because I was scared and didn't know what else to do. I'm sorry for any pain that calling them put you through." I could see that the boys were relieved. "Because you are children and not adults, I have protected you from some things so you wouldn't be hurt. So I realize how shocking this is for you both."

Chad's facade was fading but I continued. "It's important for both of you that Dad and I go to marriage counseling, but I do not feel safe here with your dad. What went on was wrong and I cannot allow you to see that behavior. Being threatened and called names is frightening to me." While the kids hung on my every word, Chad's face grew red with anger. "So, I went to see my attorney today . . ." I presented my plan and let them know I had filed for a legal separation. "If your dad does not agree to this plan, we are going to get a divorce."

Chad had heard enough. Even with witnesses at the table, he couldn't control himself. He started in with his usual mocking and sarcasm, and calling me names.

"May I interject?" Rich who is six-foot-four and a body builder, remained calm but took charge, looking at Chad. Chad nodded yes. "How you are treating your wife in front of your children right now is abusive."

Chad seethed, twisting his neck back and forth. I could tell he was barely maintaining. Then he leaned across the table and unleashed his threatening tone. "I am not leaving this house, you understand me?" And he would not agree to sign the motion. There would be no work in a batterer's group. He would not be attending a group session for adults of dysfunction. He did not need to change. He had done nothing wrong.

Rich looked at me with worry. "So where are you going to sleep tonight?"

I felt the Spirit directing me to stay. This did not sit well with Rich, who was obviously concerned for my safety. But I was resolved.

Rich turned to Chad and set some ground rules, such as, "Will Jenny be free to move about the home without you following her and intimidating her?" Chad was clearly irritated but our sons' eyes were on him. He uttered a resentful yes. Rich asked me to follow him outside and again expressed his concern. I promised to be alert and flee if I sensed danger. Before leaving, he promised that he and his wife would be praying.

I took a deep breath and walked back into my home, entrusting my life to God.

The Lion's Den

My pod started calling my house the Lion's Den. "How's the den?" they would often ask.

In one of the most amazing displays of the power of God I had ever experienced, my sons and I hung out together that first night, reconnecting and letting each other know without words that all was well between us. They held my hand, and we told jokes and watched YouTube videos. Even after that vicious character assassination by the evil one, God restored them to me. Because Jesus wins. Every time. Still, I'd have to endure Chad, who immediately dispensed with Rich's ground rules and started in with the mocking. And he insisted that when we went to our first counseling session I was to recant all my abuse allegations. Life was not going to be easy in the den.

I said goodnight to my sons, locked my bedroom door, and climbed into bed. It was hard to digest all that had taken place in a mere two days, but I knew God's Word was being proven true in my life. "For God, who said, 'Let light shine out of darkness,' made his light shine in our hearts to give us the light of the knowledge of God's glory displayed in the face of Christ. But we have this treasure in jars of clay to show that this all-surpassing power is from God and not from us. We are hard pressed on every side, but not crushed; perplexed, but not in despair; persecuted, but not abandoned; struck down, but not destroyed" (2 Corinthians 4:6–9).

My counselor let me know that how Chad had behaved in front of the children was in fact reportable abuse and that it could not continue. I told him what was in the motion and he agreed to urge Chad to sign it. Unfortunately, he never had a chance. Chad stopped going to counseling.

More and more, it was becoming painfully clear that given the choice between clinging to his wife or his sin, Chad would keep choosing sin.

While Chad waited for his new job to start, he was home twenty-four hours a day, staring me down. Often, if I decided to meet his gaze and stand firm, I did not even recognize him. It was as if something or someone else was looking at me through his eyes. They had not always looked this way. I muscled through those first few days as best as I could.

We only had one vehicle at the time, and I kept the keys on my person at all times. No way would I be left home without an escape vehicle. Now it was time for me to move forward.

One of the passages of Scripture my pod frequently prayed over me was Isaiah 61. This became my life line, and I read it daily through rivers of tears.

> The Spirit of the Sovereign LORD is on me, because the LORD has anointed me to proclaim good news to the poor. He has sent me to bind up the brokenhearted, to proclaim freedom for the captives and release from darkness for the prisoners, to proclaim the year of the LORD's favor and the day of vengeance of our God, to comfort all who mourn, and provide for those who grieve in Zion—to bestow on them a crown of beauty instead of ashes, the oil of joy instead of mourning, and a garment of praise instead of a spirit of despair. . . . Instead of your shame you will receive a double portion, and instead of disgrace you will rejoice in your inheritance. . . . I delight greatly in the LORD; my soul rejoices in my God. For he has clothed me with the garments of salvation and arrayed me in a robe of his righteousness, as a bridegroom adorns his head like a priest, and as a bride adorns herself with her jewels. (verses 1–3, 7, 10)

I bought an inexpensive silver-plated wristband and had this Scripture reference engraved on it so that throughout my day I'd be reminded of Christ's ministry to the brokenhearted. I prayed daily for discernment, and God began to reveal things to my spirit as I could handle them. In prayer with my pod every week, the Lord continued his transformative work in me.

One day when I had a tremendous sense of foreboding that I couldn't shake, I entered into this time of prayer and experienced a sudden filling of my entire body, from head to toe, with intense heat. My breath was taken away by a sense of darkness, and in my mind's eye I saw Chad kneeling on the ground. Over his head I saw a demonic being and an angelic being warring. I heard the Spirit say I should keep praying for his soul. He was close to making a decision that would destroy him. And a dark plan was being hatched against me at that very moment. Every hair on my body stood on end. My pod and I went to battle, standing up to the dark forces that were at work against Chad, binding the enemy in the mighty name of Jesus.

I had been recently restored to my father after several years apart, and he and his wife, Samantha, had become a source of comfort and strength to me during these difficult days. I called them and let them know what was happening. Turned out I hadn't needed to say a thing. The Spirit had already warned them. They too, along with my brother Thomas, were praying for Chad to be delivered from evil and for plans of darkness to be thwarted.

That night I awoke suddenly, sat straight up in bed, and looked at the clock. It was just before midnight. *Get out now!* I heard in my spirit. With my heart beating practically outside my chest, I threw on my robe, ran to the garage, and soon was speeding toward my friend Steph's. She answered her phone on one ring, met me outside of her home, and we embraced. We pulled my car into her garage so that it could not be seen. Just then I received a text message from Chad's cousin Kristen who lived three thousand miles to the east, where it was already three o'clock in the morning. "Jen, are you ok?" The Spirit had awoken her from a deep sleep and directed her to pray for me.

The next morning I learned Michelle had also been awakened and informed that I was in danger and instructed to pray for me. Steph tucked me into her guest room and we prayed for deliverance for Chad and sleep for me. After a miraculously peaceful night's sleep, I returned to the den, discerning that I had been given victory and that the plan for my physical harm had been taken off the table. At least for the moment.

We were at an impasse. Chad was completely unrepentant, and he was livid. I had drawn a line in the sand by saying that if he was not willing to work at real change by signing the court order, I was going to divorce him. The problem was that I didn't have the strength to follow through.

But one way God continued to sustain me was by telling others exactly the same things he was telling me. Especially Chad's cousin. I would often call Kristen and say, "I believe the Lord is telling me . . ." and she would have received the same word. For years Kristen had been trying to tell me that Chad's behavior was the result of rebellion to God, and that what I was experiencing in my home was spiritual in nature. Yet Chad convinced me his cousin was an over-spiritual, "demon behind every bush" weirdo. He had openly expressed disdain for her and was angered by her love for and submission to God.

Journal entry:

In my spirit I really don't believe that Chad is going to sign the court order but I pray that I am wrong. Whatever happens, God will work for my good. My hope isn't in the courts, it isn't in the order, his counselor, or anything else. I lift my eyes up to the mountain. Where does my help come from?

Chad and I interviewed a family counselor see if she could help our kids through this painful situation. After listening to Chad share his "wisdom" about how he was handling things with the boys, she said, "You can't say stuff like that to your kids!" Only she used a more crude word than "stuff." "You are aligning yourself with your sons against your wife. That is so wrong and so hurtful." Chad was furious (and of course she would not get the job). He claimed I'd faked going to the shelter and lied about everything, and there was no way he was signing the court order.

That was the slap in the face I needed to muster my courage. Right then and there in the counselor's office, I told him I was going to file for divorce. I did not respect him as a man, and every warm feeling I ever had for him had been beaten out of me. Chad sat calmly and said that he would agree to the divorce, and he desired to make the process as peaceful as possible for our sons. I was stunned and confused, but he appeared genuine.

But when we returned home, everything changed. He directed me to sit. "You listen to me," he said. His face contorted and he shook his finger in my face. "If you try to take more than 50 percent custody of the kids, it is over. And if you tell anyone about the abuse, it is over. If you do, I will take you down in flames, ruin everything you love, destroy you, and leave you penniless. Do you understand me?"

Yes, sir. Loud and clear. I promised to keep my mouth shut and never try to take his kids away from him. He promised that if I stopped the action with my attorney, we could work things out peaceably through mediation. I wanted so desperately to believe we could keep things calm for the boys that I agreed—even though Chad had been breaking his promises ever since the day we said, "I do."

Open Heart Surgery

Even while my emotions, resolve, and faith changed from day to day, God's presence remained steadfast and he ministered to me in new ways, revealing things that would prove to be life changing. I was learning that when we are walking through a crisis and there is no end in sight, if we keep our eyes focused on Christ, we will have not only survived the day but grown in some way. As the weeks turned into months without resolution to my crisis, God had a chance to perform open-heart surgery on me. And boy did I need it.

God had always spoken to me through my dreams. More than once, the thing I dreamt about ended up happening the following day, and I was prepared to handle the situation because I had been warned by the Spirit. One night during the early days of my "open-heart surgery," I had a dream that seemed massively significant.

Journal entry:

My heart is literally beating out of my chest right now. . . . In my dream Chad was waving a gun and looking at me menacingly as I drove away with the boys. We had to wind our way through sewage in an underground passageway to find him. He was possessed. I begged him to submit to Christ or else the demons would come back with even more strength and numbers. Over and over, he wouldn't submit and each time they came back his face became more contorted and scary. Finally he grew pointy teeth and took on the appearance of the demons. . . . Then came another attack. I got an email from a family member. It was so sad and so dark. I am shaking with adrenaline and feel like I could vomit. . . . There is going to be nothing ordinary about this divorce. Demonic strongholds are being destroyed and Satan doesn't like it. Well guess what? All these attacks do is strengthen my resolve. It's on, and in Christ alone I stand!

The email had also been sent to Chad. Curses hurled against us and our sons from a family member on Chad's side. I had never been confronted with such vile, hateful words—except from Chad. And then it hit me. The accusations, the tone, the reasoning. It was all so familiar because I had encountered this particular demonic presence many times in my marriage. The dark face I awoke to after many a nightmare. This message hadn't come from my family member, who knew Christ and walked with him daily. He may have typed the words and pressed send, but the message did not originate with him. The dark force operating in and around Chad was trying to get his claws into this person as well, whispering in his ear and encouraging him to write things that clearly did not come from the Spirit of God.

The revelation that Chad's behavior was in fact demonic in nature wasn't new at all, except to me. Chad's cousin had been holding the keys to my victory for a decade, and she had tried her best to hand the keys to me. But I was too beat down to listen. Yet she had remained faithful. She never stopped praying for or loving us, and never backed down from her stance that I needed to learn to put on the full armor of God every day and do battle this way.

I had limited understanding of "generational curses," specific forms of sin that affect families and are thought of as a curse because they lead to repetitive negative consequences down generational lines. The biblical basis for generational curses comes from Exodus 34:6–7. "And he passed in front of Moses, proclaiming, 'The LORD, the LORD, the compassionate and gracious God, slow to anger, abounding in love and faithfulness, maintaining love to thousands, and forgiving wickedness, rebellion and sin. Yet he does not leave the guilty unpunished; he punishes the children and their children for the sin of the parents to the third and fourth generation.'"

I could easily see the sin that had long infected my side of the family. Many had been ravaged by drug addiction and alcoholism. But there was a different stronghold on Chad's side of the family. I often heard stories of his grandfather's rage, which had been passed down and was now sitting squarely on Chad's shoulders and making my life a living hell. Who knew what had been going on behind closed doors for the last three and four generations in the name of anger? I knew one thing, though. It was going to stop with me.

This was not going to be passed to my sons. I was living under the new covenant of the blood of Christ, and that meant change was possible. Even before Christ came into the world, God spoke a new word to the Israelites through the prophet Ezekiel in chapter 18:19–20. "Yet you ask, 'Why does the son not share the guilt of his father?'. . . The child will not share the guilt of the parent, nor will the parent share the guilt of the child. The righteousness of the righteous will be credited to them, and the wickedness of the wicked will be charged against them."

Now was the time for this demonic presence to be out of a job. God didn't force me to passively lie down and accept abuse as my unavoidable reality. I had done that willingly. But wasn't it just like God to break through the manipulations that keep us bound in chains by sending forth his light and love? He had the power to take what Satan intended for my harm and turn it around. So I commanded that impure spirit to take a hike, to march his sorry, scrawny butt back to hell. *You are no longer welcome in my house and have no authority over my sons because they are covered by the blood of the Lamb.*

12

NOT FINISHED WITH ME YET

"Jennifer, is there anything the Lord has put on your heart tonight?" an elderly man from our church asked.

I'd sobbed my way through the service in which a guest speaker talked about his life of service on the mission field, and now I'd followed the line of weary souls to the front of the sanctuary for prayer. As a teen I had gone on a few summer missions and felt called to missions. But now twenty-two years of my life had passed me by, and I hadn't been used for God at all.

Tears started to flow again. "I had surrendered my life to the idea of missions as a teenager and instead lived in an abusive marriage for over twenty years. I've only recently found the strength to break free."

My confession must have shaken him. He looked at me tenderly. "Jennifer, I can't say for sure if this is from God, but I believe he is telling me that you are holding on to disappointments. He wants you to let them go. Open your hands and let them go, so he can fill them with better things."

I was stunned. I looked up at this kind man with amazement, and my tears began to wane.

"I believe he's also telling me that because he allowed this suffering in your life, you are going to have an impact for the kingdom of God that is far greater than you can fathom." Then he prayed a sweet prayer over my life. Wow. Just when I thought my pain was going to kill me, I received a healing touch by the Spirit.

Just as God was using this time to build my faith, he was also using it to reveal sin in my life and untangle my tangled thinking. A few years prior, a friend opened up to me about the latest in a long list of intolerable behaviors her husband had put her through. What she shared was vile and abusive. She was considering divorce. I was walking in such darkness at the time that I didn't offer a hug or support as other women would have. I had nursed my own suffering into a massive, steaming pile of religious pride. I told her it would be better for her children if she stayed, and that if she just submitted herself to God he could restore the marriage and help her to forgive. And I stood by silently as she muscled forward while others accused her of being selfish and a gold-digger. I had not been a safe person for her, and things were never the same between us.

Truth be told, I thought any woman who walked away from their marriage was weak in the knees, a real wuss. Until I was the one walking away. Now that I was walking in my friend's shoes and had myself been judged by others who did not know the truth of my story, the weight of the injuring sin I had committed against her crushed me. God brought her to mind and laid a heavy duty dose of conviction upon me. I needed to apologize.

I used to run into this friend all the time, but of course now that I was praying for an opportunity to see her, she was nowhere to be found. Then, on the third and final day of a fast, I was out surfing alone, which was a miracle in itself because the beach break I was surfing was usually packed with people. God always seemed to do something remarkable during my fasts, and I was waiting expectantly. And then my friend paddled right up beside me and said hello with a gracious smile I didn't deserve. My heart beat a little faster and harder, the way it does when the Spirit is prompting me to do something scary. After some small talk, I summoned the courage.

"I have actually been hoping I'd see you."

"Oh?" She looked worried, and I sensed she was bracing herself for whatever hurtful thing might come out of my mouth.

"I have been going through some things . . . God is doing open-heart surgery on me. And I just want you to know that I'm sorry I didn't support you when you were getting a divorce. I judged you in my heart, and it was so wrong."

She started crying, And I knew the pain in her face was caused by me. "That means so much to me," she said with relief—and the beginnings of healing. "You have no idea what my life has been like and what people have said."

"Actually, I do. Now I am the one being talked about. That advice I gave you when you confided in me was bad advice, from a wounded person. I hope you can forgive me." And there we were. Two women in the middle of the ocean, connected by the pain of abuse, being loved on and restored to wholeness by Jesus.

I now realized how much power each one of us holds. We hold the power to hurt and the power to heal. I vowed that day to do everything I could to be a healer.

A New Thing

"I am not going to lie. My credit is total crap," I told the loan officer candidly.

After our first mediation session, during which Chad announced that he would not be paying any of the six-thousand-dollar fee for mediation yet conceded that I could buy him out of the house so that our sons could remain in the home, I found myself in the bank seeking a refinance. My expectations were low. Less than six months earlier, I had applied for a low-limit credit card at a dumpy electronics store and been declined—in front of a crowd. So humiliating. But my father had given me the advice to remain immovable in Christ, so here I was.

Ahead of mediation, my lawyer, Leslie, gave me some bad news over the phone. Even when there were multiple trips to jail on record and multiple beatings reported, the courts did not often rule favorably for abused wives. And they were not going to just let me walk away. My reward for working two jobs and saving our house would likely be paying child and spousal support. I would have to give Chad half of my retirement if he requested it, and of course, in order to keep the house, I would need to buy him out. "Well," I said softly to the Lord while trying on a dress for an upcoming wedding, "it is totally impossible. I can't do it. So, if it works out, I will know without a doubt that it is you working." I'd hung up, feeling neither sad nor discouraged. If God was leading me out, he was going to make a way.

Chad told the mediator that despite all the havoc I was wreaking on the family, he wanted me and the boys to be able to stay in the house. He was willing to allow me to seek a refinance and forego child and spousal support.

But could I qualify for a refinance? Even though I had us back on track and was paying bills on time, our default and unsecured debt history had obliterated my credit score. Without a doubt, this would take a miracle. The loan officer said he couldn't make any promises.

But less than twenty-four hours later I received an email from him. "Well Jennifer, it looks like you are preapproved for a thirty-year, fixed rate of 3.875 percent." And there was more good news! My monthly payment would decrease by twelve hundred dollars—to the penny, the amount Chad had been contributing to the mortgage. I could do it! I received total approval and the loan was funded in record time. To quote the loan officer, "This thing is flying through!" This was Favor with a capital F.

Even though I was securing a loan on my own, and I would be the only one on the note, Chad would still be on the deed until we signed our judgment. In order for the loan to close, we needed his signature. And—surprise—he wasn't cooperating. And we were still living under the same roof.

Journal entry:

I am in the middle of a fast and not feeling very strong at all. The Lord is telling me that if I put my faith in Chad I am doomed to suffer horrible anxiety. From a human perspective, Chad has all the power right now. Fortunately, I have the Lord God Almighty fighting for me and I must look to him alone. Heavenly Father, I ask you to continue to lead me safely out of this situation and into the glorious freedom you have waiting for me.

I stepped out of my car to check the surf.

"Man, you are so radiant right now." Pastor Blaine flashed me a big smile. Since the day we met in Michelle's garage, he had been helping me walk through this dark time, and now here he was arriving at the beach at the same moment.

"Oh, hey!" I said, surprised to see him.

"No offense," he went on, "but when we first met you looked like a zombie. And now you are just shining with the Spirit." I wasn't offended. I knew that I had, in fact, looked very much like a zombie when we had our first meeting. Back then, my counselor had also told me I looked like a trauma victim.

I told Pastor Blaine I'd been wavering lately, sometimes overcome by the difficulty of looking ahead.

"Don't romanticize abuse," he cautioned me bluntly. "I know it is what you are used to and what you are comfortable living in. But when you are in the darkness, Satan's got you right where he wants you. When you are in the light, you become Satan's enemy because God is going to use you for the kingdom. You gotta keep fighting."

He was right. I was not about to turn back now, and I wasn't going to despise the miracles God was performing on my behalf. How bad could a few more weeks be? Although Chad had relocated to a room upstairs and promised to move out as soon as the refinance went through, he'd been seizing every opportunity to intimidate and provoke me. Whenever he tried, I'd obey the Spirit's whispered, *Retreat! Retreat!* and lock my bedroom door behind me. But he was becoming more bold, even barging into my room in his underwear.

That day I read these verses: "Forget the former things; do not dwell on the past. See, I am doing a new thing! Now it springs up; do you not perceive it? I am making a way in the wilderness and streams in the wasteland"(Isaiah 43:18–19). *Okay. I get it. I can do it.*

A song my son introduced me to by NEEDTOBREATHE became my battle cry during this time, and it helped me gather courage. The lyrics inspired me to "soldier on, headstrong into the storm," never looking back. It reminded me that the "first days of the war" were gone, and God was turning the tide.[1]

The song is called "Keep Your Eyes Open," and that's what I was learning to do. As much as I wanted my trials to end, they'd continue until the Spirit had completed his intended work in me. The worship and teaching I was experiencing in my new Spirit-filled church blew my mind, healed my wounds, and fueled me for battle.

Journal entry:

Holy guacamole what a service! I got socked with the Holy Spirit so heavy tonight and he ministered to me and revealed things to me in an hour and a half of intense worship. As we sang the Spirit revealed to me why rejection from people has been hitting me so hard. I have a deep-seated need for approval that comes from the little girl in me who was not loved. I never really dealt with that pain . . . . I asked Jesus to heal me of those hurts and wept so hard I shook. Then the Spirit allowed me to see how judgmental I've been in my spirit and how much pain I've caused others. . . . I could barely stand under the weight of it. I felt his forgiveness and a reminder of how it feels to be judged and to never do that to others again.

Lord, thank you for healing the little girl with the sad, sad memories.

As long as Christ approved of me and my actions, that would be good enough. No matter what people said about me.

A few days later, I leapt from my chair at the mediation table. "You're a maniac!" I yelled. "And I'm not going to live with your tyranny any longer!"

Chad had flipped a switch, not only refusing to sign the judgment we'd previously agreed upon, but substantially altering the financial terms. He was now demanding child support and spousal support. Two months had gone by since my night in the shelter. Unbeknownst to me, Chad had hired an attorney. He had no plans to peacefully settle this thing. When he got up in my face, I told him to back off and commanded him not to touch me. Needless to say, the entire mediation blew up.

Going into this meeting, my pod and I were all prayed up, so why had I lost my cool?

When I told the story to my counselor, she helped me see that how I behaved was actually appropriate. Cowering in fear was the behavior of a battered wife. I had changed my way of relating to my abuser! The Spirit had been with me during mediation. In his power, I had stood up to Chad.

Journal entry:

I've come to the place where I need to relinquish my personal belongings to a person who has contempt for me. I cannot let my personal belongings become an idol to me. Neither can I buy my way out of abuse. I have always been concerned with the idolatry and materialism of which I am a part as someone living the American dream, and now is my chance to prove that I am willing to live simply. If God wants to bless me financially he will do so, but I will not look to possessions for support or rescue.

The bank was getting antsy. They didn't like home loans just "sitting," and I got word that if I did not sign by the end of the week, I was going to have to start the entire process over. All I needed was one signature from Chad. So once again I cried out to the Lord and he answered. I asked Chad if he would be willing to allow the refinance to go through without the judgment being signed, and by the power of the Almighty God, he said yes. I immediately called my loan officer. "Give me a call when the papers are ready," I said.

A week later, my loan officer introduced me to another manager and told her the story of my unlikely loan. "It's because she prayed," he added. And I could tell he believed it. We had never discussed religion, but I could see how others were being touched by the power of God. Faith was being built up in others as well as in me. Chad maintained his state of "temporary sanity" until three days later, when it was too late to change his mind, saying he "never should have allowed me to refinance." Although I was so thankful for the victory, every time something like this happened, living in the den became that much more precarious and oppressive.

A few days later, I was back in the bank, helping my son open a teen checking account. The bank clerk politely chatted with us as she brought up my file. My loan had funded, she said, and I qualified for a free checking account upgrade. Also, I had been preapproved for a credit card.

I wrinkled my nose. "I don't think that's right."

She looked at her computer screen. "It says right here that you are preapproved. Would you like to apply? I can't promise much, and it may take a few days." I held my breath while her fingers furiously typed. "Wow!" she said, looking surprised and pleased.

"What?" I asked, trying to appear calm.

"This hardly ever happens. You have been instantly approved for the maximum amount."

I just about fell out of my chair. "How much is that?"

"Six thousand dollars."

This got my son's attention. "We're rich!" he exclaimed. While she collected the paperwork from the printer, I explained to him that the six thousand dollars was not real money and we certainly weren't rich, but that it was a good feeling to have the trust of the bank. I looked up and smiled toward heaven. Favor. Blessing. A double portion for my shame.

No Condemnation

"You should have seen her before—she is literally a new creation!" Michelle's husband told the guest pastor. "God has done such a work in her!" I seemed to be the poster child for the goodness and power of God.

So at his and Michelle's urging, I went ahead and gave my testimony at the prayer service. I shared about how the Spirit had warned me when Chad threatened to kill me. About purchasing life insurance and drawing up a will and being resigned to death. About my vision in the safe house, the spiritual warfare, and how God had thwarted a plan for my harm. I shared about my financial restoration and how now, through the power of God, I knew I was going to live. Everyone rejoiced. My pod was beaming over me.

After the pastor led us in a general prayer session, he asked if anyone needed prayer. I requested the group specifically pray that Chad would move out of the home for my safety. My friend Jamie picked up her oil and prepared to anoint me for prayer. But then the vibe changed.

"I could never pray for your husband to move out," said the guest pastor. "All divorce is from Satan." The room fell silent. I felt all the blood draining from my body—except my cheeks, which were hot with the sting of humiliation.

"But he has been abusing her for twenty-two years and he's threatened to kill her," one of my friends said.

"No. God desires to restore all marriages."

A girl I barely knew came and stood by me, looking pained on my behalf. My pod pled my case, to no avail. I tried to speak up for myself. "That's not right," I said. "God is leading me in this. I have not been unfaithful to Chad or to God's Word."

I drove home stunned, horrified, and physically shaking. In my room, I stood still, trying to comprehend what had happened. It took all my energy to stay upright and not collapse under the weight of my humiliation. What unfolded next is difficult to describe. I will do my best. Beneath me, the wood floor had changed to dirt. To my right were people wearing long robes, as if I was in some sort of Bible scene. In their hands, they all held stones. And I instantly discerned that I was identifying with the adulterous woman in the New Testament. She—or I?—was about to be stoned to death. And then something amazing happened. I saw myself simply step past the leader of the group and fall into the arms of Christ. He was there. I saw and felt him. I pressed my face into his chest, and he stroked my hair and held me like a child. "There is no condemnation for you," he whispered. "I am your Good Shepherd and you hear my voice."

The vision left me feeling loved. Whole. Guilt-free. Shame-free. I didn't need to ask my pastor or my pod if I was doing the right thing. I was loved by Jesus. And this was the greatest miracle so far.

I had spent most of my life striving to earn God's favor yet never feeling like I quite measured up. But now I'd been sucker-punched by the law in front of a crowd, and I felt nothing but loved. I felt no anger toward the pastor. Remember that woman who at one time was incapable of empathy when her friend came to her for support? That had been me, so sure that I was the righteous one. But now I understood, through my journey out of the darkness, that there is a religious spirit that does not come from God. It attacks, and it deceives blood-bought Christians. I once hadn't recognized that spirit at work in me, when I crushed my friend, and now this pastor did not recognize it was at work in him, in declaring my testimony invalid with his refusal to pray for me.

My thoughts were now centered around my great God, and I praised him for the healing work he had done in me and for ministering to me in such a profound way. He allowed me to experience humiliation for a reason. It too would be a powerful part of my testimony, and he would use it for his glory. I had been a stone-thrower many times in my life. Now I knew what it felt like to be on the other side, and I vowed never to pick up another stone.

Six months had passed since God revealed himself to me in the safe house. Although there had been many days I wished God would simply rescue me, I was coming to cherish what I called my time "in the desert." Think what I would have missed! Each morning, I grabbed a cup of hot coffee, sat at the kitchen table, and met with Jesus. I couldn't believe all the years I'd wasted, "too busy" for this beautiful, life-saving time of communion.

I now understood that I didn't have to earn God's love or favor. Those things already belonged to me. I had once been such a know-it-all, giving out advice quickly. Now I knew that I didn't know jack squat. And I was learning to surrender, to grasp that my life wasn't about me at all. It was about my Jesus. My bridegroom. My Abba. My portion. I had come to desire his presence above anything else he could give. The light of Christ had crashed through my darkness and was healing me in tangible ways. God was good, and he could be trusted.

Beauty for Ashes

I went to work the following day, elated. Even if seeing visions made me sound like a total nutcase, I had to share with a few close friends about Christ's love. But about six hours in, I started coughing and it became clear I was getting sick. I was thankful to be released early and headed home, although this would mean more time in the den, which I dreaded. When I pulled up, Chad was chatting good-naturedly with a neighbor, but when the neighbor left Chad turned and gave me his I-hate-you glare and got into his car. I spotted my son hanging out in the garage with a friend and let him know his aunt and uncle would be visiting that night.

"I'm spending the night at Dad's," he said. "He has a condo."

That is odd, I thought. After a heated exchange, in which Chad asserted that I would never be allowed to even come near his new place to pick the boys up, he screeched out of the driveway and was gone.

What exactly was going on? The full impact didn't hit me until I went upstairs and opened the door to Chad's bedroom. His stuff was gone. He had moved out. For six months, I had been praying that my abuser would move out. And God, in his wisdom and power, chose to answer that prayer the day after a pastor had refused to pray for me. I was speechless. And now I found myself alone, realizing I had focused so long on breaking free from my abusive husband's oppression but never really considered how I would feel when it happened.

I started cleaning the house to prepare for my sister's visit. But while I was putting the silverware away, the Holy Spirit came on me in power and I realized . . . the demonic presence was gone. There was no darkness, nothing to battle. It had left with him and would never return. My house was already "clean."

I started to weep. But these were tears of joy. "You did it! You stopped the violence! I'm alive! And you're here! You didn't leave me!" I twirled around the living room—*my* living room. "I was in such a pit, with no way out! I was in such darkness, but you did it!" I laughed and cried and leapt for joy. I dropped to my knees on the throw rug in my living room and raised my hands to heaven. Every time I tried to compose myself and move on, I could not stop praising.

Later that evening I realized that God had answered his promises to me from Isaiah 61 through the visitation of the Spirit. He had given me a crown of beauty for my ashes and the oil of gladness for my mourning. He had given me a spirit of praise for a spirit of despair. God in his great mercy was fulfilling his promises to me.

Even while my life was falling apart.

13

DOMINION

hat if the mere mention of Jesus Christ's name was enough to send demons running for the hills? It only took me forty-three years to figure this out, but once I did, my life began to radically change. And here's the thing: this power and protection is available to every Spirit-filled Christian.

In case you are raising your eyebrows and thinking to yourself, "I am not sure about all this demon stuff," I would like to offer proof from Scripture why I believe demons are not only real but at work in the world today. Think about it. It is considered perfectly fine to talk about the existence of angelic beings—of guardian angels and how angels protect us. Angels grace the covers of books and calendars. Wearing an angel pendant will not garner a sideways glance.

But bring up the existence of demonic beings, and some people may wonder if perhaps the doctor needs to increase the dosage of your medication. And commanding demons? That could be considered going too far. Why the disparity? God's Word exposes and illuminates this deception, which I believe in itself is perpetuated by Satan. But don't take my word for it. I encourage you to seek out theologians and to look into these matters for yourself. Through intensive study of God's Word and daily prayers for discernment, God has revealed much to this ordinary disciple. I know he will do the same for you.

And this knowledge is an important weapon of warfare when dealing with people who may be subject to evil influences. I am in the medical profession, and in no way am I suggesting that all mental illness and disease is a manifestation of demonic oppression. Jesus taught that things happen for different reasons. Some diseases are the consequences of sin—we are a fallen people living in a fallen world—while others are allowed so that the works of God might be displayed (see John 9:3). But clearly, Jesus healed some people with mental and physical ailments that were due to demonic possession. And these weren't all witchcraft-practicing occult members. The people in the Gospels who were affected by demons were average, ordinary citizens. Even Mary Magdalene. Even people in the church.

If angels of God exist, angels of Satan exist as well. Here's an example from the book of Job: "On another day the angels came to present themselves before the LORD, and Satan also came with them to present himself before him. And the LORD said to Satan, 'Where have you come from?' Satan answered the LORD, 'From roaming throughout the earth, going back and forth on it'" (Job 2:1–2).

In biblical times, the fact that demons existed and that they were at work in and around communities was commonly known and accepted. Everyone from the religious elite to society's poor knew this to be true. From Matthew 9:34: "But the Pharisees said, 'It is by the prince of demons that he drives out demons.'" And from Matthew 15:22: "A Canaanite woman from that vicinity came to him, crying out, 'Lord, son of David, have mercy on me! My daughter is demon-possessed and suffering terribly.'" These are just a fraction of the verses that speak about demons and their influence on humans.[1] The presence of the demonic can manifest as self-mutilation, loss of speech, out-of-control behavior, and an inability to live peacefully with others. Sounds a lot like things going on in our modern world, although we have other names for them such as cutting and antisocial personality disorder.

Many times when I looked at Chad, what I saw behind his eyes looking back at me was not of this world. Yet even people who are severely given over to demonic oppression are not without hope. Somewhere deep inside, there is a soul that *can* be saved! Jesus was able to deliver and restore even the most radically possessed, because underneath the screaming, foaming at the mouth, and fits of rage was a human soul that only the Spirit of God could reach. This is why Chad could do both good and evil things within the same day. There were moments he was able to relate to me in a sane, respectful manner. But when he urged the young wife he had vowed to love and cherish to turn a loaded gun on herself, the demonic was manifested.

You may ask, How do demons gain influence and power over Christians? I had wondered this myself. How could Chad be a loving father and a helpful neighbor and yet be under demonic influence? In an instant, he could change and manifest violence, threats, and rage. Think about Judas Iscariot. Judas spent countless hours with Jesus and the other disciples. Scripture doesn't disclose why in the world Judas would choose darkness when he was an eyewitness to the life and ministry of Jesus. But clearly, simply being part of a Christian community doesn't automatically protect us from being given over to the enemy's activity.

I'm sure the first time Judas took a little something from the treasury bag, he never imagined he would become the Lord's betrayer. Like Judas, we are each given a free will, with the power to choose who we are going to serve. Possession involves mastery and captivity. In other words, we are captive to whoever has mastery over us. "Don't you know that when you offer yourselves to someone as obedient slaves, you are slaves of the one you obey—whether you are slaves to sin, which leads to death, or to obedience which leads to righteousness?" (Romans 6:16). "They promise them freedom, while they themselves are slaves of depravity—for 'people are slaves to whatever has mastered them'" (2 Peter 2:19).

I was coming to understand with absolute certainty that the only reason I was still in my home and Chad was living in a condo down the street was because the demonic forces operating in and around him had to bow to the authority of Jesus Christ. Period.

The first time I went to Chad's condo to pick up my sons, I decided to bring my brother-in-law along. Our family has given my brother-in-law two nicknames—the Holy Spirit, and Job. We call him the Holy Spirit because he is full of peace, joy, kindness, and all the Fruits of the Spirit. We call him Job because of all the injuries and losses he has endured yet remained faithful to God. Once, someone asked him, "Why are you so happy all the time?"

"What do I have to be sad about?" he answered. We could all learn a little something from hanging with this guy, and that is why I asked him to come with me. But he ended up being more like a guardian against evil. Pulling up to the condo, Lee and I were both instantly subjected to Chad's vicious wrath. Chad even reached into the car and struck him several times. Lee did not retaliate. Later he said the Holy Spirit told him to turn the other cheek.

The boys came home angry and oppositional. We spent the next few days rebuilding what had been destroyed by hate and loving them back to health. Several nights later, the front door swung open and Chad marched in. He terrorized my sister. I melted in fear at his sinister words and demeanor. We had to get the police involved. All my spiritual warfare training had flown out the window and I felt worthless and defeated.

Michelle led the pod in prayer over me, and she had stern words for me. "You have reverted back to your covenant with fear. That was broken. You are now under the blood covenant of Jesus. When Chad is standing in the street, yelling at you like a crazy person, that is a demonic manifestation, and you have dominion over that. His moving out was a huge victory. He kept you isolated in order to continue the evil of his abuse, and now when the demons see a physical show of the support you have, they're flipping out in anger. They don't like seeing your sister with you. But nothing has changed. God is still God. You need to look right at Chad and rebuke that in the name of Jesus. Don't forget who you are in Christ."

She was so right. I had returned to my old thinking and way of responding. I accepted her gentle rebuke. I picked myself up, brushed the dirt off my jeans, and set my eyes on Jesus.

The next couple of exchanges weren't much better, and each time my sons returned they were disrespectful and angry. They had always been such good, loving boys, and I knew they were in turmoil. I remembered that in the book I'd read about abuse, the author instructed battered women to demand respect at all times from their children, and to be the best parent they could be. So I called my sons out whenever they were disrespectful, and they were always filled with remorse and apologetic. This was not their fault. And it was time to adopt a new plan.

When the next time came for the kids to go to Chad's, I issued a command, rendering the demons ineffective—in the powerful name of Jesus. When I arrived to pick them up a few days later, I commanded the demons to remain silent. And when the boys got in the car I knew immediately that the dominion I had been given was real. They were not angry, nor was there a hint of disrespect. I was beginning a practice that would become a way of peace for myself and my children in a time of chaos, and it allowed them to continue to have a relationship with their dad.

Not an Equal Opponent

The abuse of women and children is vile sin and an affront to God. If a man continues to be an abuser and does not repent of this willful disobedience, he opens himself up to demonic oppression. He can be taken captive by Satan. Chad seemed genuinely remorseful at the beginning of our relationship, but as he continued to walk in the sin of abuse, and refused to repent, his heart became hard. He was given over to darkness. Scripture teaches that as we continue to walk in disobedience, God may give us over to a depraved mind. "Furthermore, just as they did not think it worthwhile to retain the knowledge of God, so God gave them over to a depraved mind, so that they do what ought not to be done" (Romans 1:28) Therefore we are warned, "Be alert and of sober mind. Your enemy the devil prowls around like a roaring lion looking for someone to devour" (1 Peter 5:8). Satan was devouring Chad's life.

But there was and is hope. "Opponents must be gently instructed, in the hope that God will grant them repentance leading them to a knowledge of the truth, and that they will come to their senses and escape from the trap of the devil, who has taken them captive to do his will" (2 Timothy 2:25–26).

At one time, I would have been scared to write about demons. But to the Christian who has been sealed with the blood of the Lamb and filled with the Spirit of God, they are pathetic, insignificant, creatures of doom. They know their fate is sealed and tremble at the name of Christ. Are they good at what they do? Of course—they have been at it for a long, long time. Do we as believers have the power to overcome their schemes? Oh, yes, we do! "The seventy-two returned with joy and said, 'Lord, even the demons submit to us in your name.'" Jesus' brother wrote to us, "Submit yourselves, then, to God. Resist the devil, and he will flee from you" (James 4:7). Luke tells us that Jesus is so powerful that when handkerchiefs and aprons that had touched the apostle Paul were taken to the sick, the demons left them and they were healed (Acts 19:12).

Demons are our enemies, but they are not an equal opponent. It is not us against them. It is the Spirit of Christ in us against them. We have dominion because Jesus has been given dominion (see Colossians 1:11–18). In his letter to the Ephesians, Paul wrote that he wanted us to know we possessed Jesus' "incomparably great power for us who believe. That power is the same as the mighty strength he exerted when he raised Christ from the dead and seated him at his right hand in the heavenly realms, far above rule and authority, power and dominion, and every name that is invoked, not only in the present age but also in the one to come" (Ephesians 1:18–21).

Chad let me know he had come into the house and taken all of the family photos and kids' baby pictures off the walls, saying he planned to make copies and give them back. But he never did. As time passed I grieved the loss of these precious memories and the fact that there was nothing I could do about it. But then again, maybe there was. One morning as I arrived to pick up the boys, I prayed, "Father, you say if I ask anything in accordance with your will in the name of Jesus it will be given to me. I really want my pictures back." And then I took dominion.

"Demons, I want my pictures put into a box and placed in the back of my car! In the name of Jesus, it will be done!" I knocked on Chad's door, opened the trunk, and hurried back to the front seat. Lo and behold, as I sat listening to praise music, Chad came marching outside carrying a box with the pictures inside. He placed it in the trunk, turned, and walked away. Dominion.

14

Facing My Truth

It was Christmas morning. Beautiful, wondrous Christmas. I'd awoken early to keep my standing appointment with Jesus at the kitchen table before setting off for work, and here I sat. Rejoicing as never before. Weeping tears of joy and gratitude for the gift of Christ and what his birth meant for me. I still had many battles ahead, but that didn't matter. I was alive because Jesus was born to die for me. Out of the darkness, into the light. What a glorious Christmas indeed.

Despite Chad's latest attacks, attempts to undermine my relationship with my sons, and legal trickery, the boys were not merely surviving but showing signs of joy amid turmoil. We had spent Christmas Eve together at my friend Steph's house, enjoying a big dinner and surrounded by a boisterous family. My sons and I had come home, taken communion together, and opened presents. They'd hugged me and said it was our best Christmas yet, and I could tell they meant it.

Recently I had been navigating doubts. *Had God really said I was allowed to leave my marriage? Is this outcome really worth seeing my sons go back and forth between two homes—something I once swore I would never put them through? If only Chad had simply committed adultery, so I wouldn't have to wrestle with these thoughts. Then I could just grab onto the "escape clause" in the gospel and get away without having to exercise an ounce of faith. But if all this wasn't of God's leading, if I've been out of his will, why am I experiencing his presence more powerfully now than in my entire life? And what about the vision in the safe house? And all the specific things he spoke to me that came true? And what about the miracles?*

What if I changed my mind?

My teenage sons would learn that this was how they could treat their wives, no matter how badly they themselves behaved, even if they were unrepentant. They'd learn that women are weak and will eventually cave in and take them back. And they would learn that spousal abuse is just fine with God. If I turned back now, my sons would be left to believe that all my newfound strength in the Spirit and love for Jesus was just the temporary ravings of an insane mother—just like their dad had claimed all along.

No, I had decided. There was too much at stake and I had come too far. I would not go back to the darkness. Perhaps these doubts were flaming arrows being hurled in my direction because I was on the verge of a breakthrough. Only God knew. But for now, I would hold tightly onto my shield of faith, yield myself completely to God's plan, and march forward into my new destiny in Christ—without any idea how I would get there. I wasn't in the middle of the storm because I had sinned or because I was out of God's will. I was here because Jesus told me to get into the boat and go the other side.

I muscled through my shift on Christmas Day, the first Christmas I'd ever spent apart from my sons. This was just how our visitation days turned out, and I was left to muddle through without them for the next five days. Bitterness and resentment reared their ugly heads. By the fourth day, I was feeling very weighed down and discouraged. My work called to say they were overstaffed and to ask if I would like the day off. Just what the doctor ordered. I surfed for two hours in conditions that normally would have put a perma-grin on my face for the rest of the day, yet my heart remained heavy. Then a trip to the mailbox about did me in.

In response to our most recent mediation effort, in which the Holy Spirit came upon me and I told Chad that I would no longer hold back the truth, I'd received another fat envelope full of lies, well-crafted by his attorney. My friend Barb had given Chad a large loan, big enough to cover attorney fees so he could make good on his promise to "take me down in flames and leave me penniless."

I'd been hearing the horror stories unfolding around me about other women in my community who were being destroyed in the courts. One had been accused by her husband of having an affair. Her upper-middle-class husband took a baseball bat to her head as she slept, and put her in the intensive care unit. Because he was wealthy, he was able to drain his retirement fund and post a million dollars bail and was out of jail. Meanwhile, she was in hiding. Another woman I knew had recently broken a window and jumped out of it with her three babies in order to escape her abuser's violent attack. When she returned to the home to get some important documents for the kids, the abuser called the police. "So you're the one who broke the window," the police officer scolded harshly. When she tried to explain that she was escaping from a violent attack, the officer replied, "I don't care if he beats you black and blue every day. You have no right to keep his kids from him!" And another woman whose husband was a police officer was seeking divorce because he had been soliciting prostitutes. But in court, the judge ruled favorably for the husband.

On my better days, I knew better than to put my hope in a judge, the legal system, the police, or in my own strength. I was to put my hope in the Lord God Almighty. Still, I cast the papers aside and fell down on my bed, sobbing.

When, God, are you going to vindicate me? To borrow a line from King David, "How long must I mourn the oppression of my enemies?" Why was I was paying the consequences for Chad's rebellion? In desperation, I phoned my sister for encouragement. Then Steph, who prayed with me. And finally Michelle, who mentioned that a Christian conference was being streamed live via the internet. It couldn't hurt. I still felt like giving up but decided to check it out.

A young woman took the stage and began playing the piano, singing words given by the Spirit, words from God's heart to his children. They went something like this: "I see the beginning and the end. You see a fail-ure, and I see an overcomer. You see fear, but I see courage. If you don't quit, you are going to win. . . . It won't be that much longer. I am going to make everything beautiful, and the truth is going to be told." I wept at the goodness of God. I had been so concerned about my sons, and she had a word for that too. "Fathers are broken but I am bigger than that. Your babies are my babies. Your children are my children. I am bigger than any mistake you think you have made."

Once again the Spirit reached out to me in the depths of my despair and proved himself to be faithful when I was faithless. Eating was again hard for me, but I gagged down some toast and called it a night. Despite the Spirit's words to me, peace escaped me and I lay awake. Then I had an epiphany. Chad had written lies, but I could tell the truth. And because it was truth, I could substantiate it. I got out of bed, turned on my laptop, and wrote a response to Chad's declaration. There in print was my life with him in abbreviated form, and it was horrifying to read. This was more direct and specific than the testimony I had given in my previous declaration.

Now I had peace. I was capable and intelligent and I could build a rock-solid case for my truth—police reports, phone records, a record from the shelter. Perhaps I could find the therapist who saw me when I was a terrified young bride. And I had my family members, who could write a statement on my behalf. It was going to be all right.

What Chad was doing now—dragging me into court for more money, inventing lies, and turning my friends against me—these were all things Bancroft described in his book. It was as if Chad had a copy of the book and was using it to plan his next move. In chapter 11 the author describes how abusive men work to succeed in getting a woman's friends and family to side with him. Indeed, the betrayal of my dear friend Barb had both surprised and hurt me deeply. Mr. Bancroft asserts that "When people take a neutral stand between you and your abusive partner, they are in effect supporting him and abandoning you, no matter how much they may claim otherwise."[1] Also, an abuser sees the legal system as another opportunity for manipulation and uses the courts to continue his abuse of the victim.

Among other things, the Spirit was preparing my heart for the possibility that my friend might witness against me in court.

15

But Am I Worthy?

One of the benefits of having to wait and see that the Lord is good is that he can (and will!) prune us while we await his rescue. But at this point, I was already feeling pretty pruned—down to a stub. The question I now found myself wrestling with was, *Am I worth it?* I was a nobody, a nothing. Would God continue to exert his mighty power on my behalf?

I was no Abraham or Sarah or Joseph or Moses. Did I dare approach God with confidence like King David's when he wrote the eighteenth Psalm?

> My God is my rock, in whom I take refuge, my shield and the horn of my salvation, my stronghold. I called to the Lord, who is worthy of praise, and I have been saved from my enemies. The cords of death entangled me; the torrents of destruction overwhelmed me. The cords of the grave coiled around me; the snares of death confronted me. In my distress I called to the Lord; I cried to my God for Help. From his temple he heard my voice; my cry came before him, into his ears. The earth trembled and quaked, and the foundations of the mountains shook; they trembled because he was angry. Smoke rose from his nostrils;

consuming fire came from his mouth, burning coals blazed out of it. He parted the heavens and came down; dark clouds were under his feet. He mounted the cherubim and flew; he soared on the wings of the wind. . . . He brought me out into a spacious place; he rescued me because he delighted in me. The Lord has dealt with me according to my righteousness; according to the cleanness of my hands he has rewarded me. For I have kept the ways of the Lord; I am not guilty of turning from my God. . . . Praise be to my Rock! Exalted be God my savior! He is the God who avenges me, who subdues nations under me, who saves me from my enemies. You exalted me above my foes; from a violent man you rescued me. Therefore I will praise you, Lord, among the nations; I will sing the praises of your name. (Psalm 18:2–9, 19–23, 46–49)

Truth be told, God had already done all these things for me, and more. Could it be that he delighted in me just as he delighted in David? I wasn't always so sure. I certainly wasn't completely blameless before him.

My attorney had informed me that most of the evidence I gathered would not be allowed by the court, and that written statements from family members would also not suffice. They would have to come and testify in person. My heart sank. My loved ones all knew the potential for Chad's violence, and no one wanted to be the final straw that made him snap. I could not ask them to risk their lives. It just wasn't worth it for an issue like spousal support. I simply had to trust the Lord to provide, no matter what the court ordered. My only goal was to complete my journey out of the darkness by boldly declaring the truth, because that was what God was calling me to do.

A New Destiny

Michelle asked if I would share my story in front of her church. But I didn't want to stand before others as the knucklehead who stayed in abuse for twenty-two years. I didn't want to be the divorced chick with unanswered prayers and a failed marriage on my resume. That was who I was. But that was not my testimony.

My testimony was that Jesus is real, and he does what he came to do.

By now I was also sure that when we are surrendered to God completely, open to doing his will, he will tuck *his* desires inside our hearts. And these are the desires he readily says yes to (see Psalm 37:4). My new desires now included telling others about the things God had done for me, and writing this book. I sensed he was going to open doors of ministry to me. The idea that he would use my suffering to help others genuinely brought comfort.

I had a powerful story to share even though I was still in the middle of the storm. Nevertheless as the time approached to share my story, I became consumed with anxiety and a strange feeling I could not put my finger on. I wasn't worried about speaking in public. I did have some concerns about what Chad warned he would do to me if I didn't remain silent, but I had come to believe that God was bigger than his threats.

I took a deep breath and stepped up to the microphone. As I surveyed the audience and prepared to speak my truth in public for the very first time, the Lord revealed the source of my anxiety. It was pride. The testimony that he had given me was not the one that I wanted. I wanted to look amazing and spiritual and for others to say, "Wow, look how great she is." Deep inside, in my flesh, I clung to their approval of me, believing it might heal the little girl in me who felt worthless.

I had endured some really heavy stuff as a child—sexual molestation, neglect, and extreme poverty, among other things. Over the years, when people learned about it and saw what a seemingly functional, emotionally well person I was, they talked about how I had "overcome," "made better choices for myself," and "turned it all around." I soaked it in and told them I gave all the glory to God. But all the while I was living a lie, pretending that I had made better choices for myself when in reality I had not.

And now I realized that the ministry I was imagining for myself was also founded on pride. I was hoping that, given the admiration of thousands of people, I could maybe, just maybe, finally look that hurting little girl in the face and say, "See that? You really are lovable. You aren't defective, and this proves it."

I thanked God for giving me this revelation right when I needed it, and I was able to share my testimony, *with all humility*, for the first time. My pod members beamed as I spoke. Some cried. Afterward, some of the believers approached me to say how thankful they were God had rescued me and to encourage me to hold my ground. They weren't blown away by how spiritual I was. My testimony was only powerful because through one real-life story, a story of heartbreak, failure, and broken dreams, the undeniable love and power of Jesus was displayed.

But I wondered if anyone had actually related to what I shared. And then I saw her. A teenager with big eyes, watching me with a hint of curiosity mixed with typical teenage aloofness. She was pregnant, and the father of the baby was a man more than twice her age. A man responsible for luring her into prostitution, selling her body for a profit, and beating her face in. A man who she still thought she loved very much.

It hit me like a punch in the gut. God had not given me a desire for ministry in my heart so I could become a card-carrying member of some kind of Christian powerhouse club. And not so I could feed my delicate ego. He placed this desire in my heart because I had been healed, and now it was time for me to bring the healer to the hurting. Jesus said it is not the well who need a doctor, but the sick. I had been "sick" for over two decades and my disease almost killed me.

I would preach the good news to the teenager with the big eyes and anyone else God brought into my life. One little lost lamb at a time.

16

WILL THE REAL ME PLEASE STAND UP

As a young girl living in a home full of turmoil, I dreamt of the day I would finally be on my own. I imagined a beautiful life for myself and thought I knew the right formula for achieving it. I would go to church, live a moral life, marry a Christian man, and be blessed with happiness. My husband and I would be devoted to one another and serve the Lord together. Marriage would be hard work, but with love all things were possible.

While coming to grips with the reality of my current situation, I met a young girl in Scripture to whom I could relate. Her name was Hagar. Her life wasn't very beautiful either. She was a slave girl, given as a concubine to Abraham. She wasn't exactly thrilled when she turned up pregnant and was forced to flee due to mistreatment. I knew what it was like to be mistreated, and I knew what it felt like to flee. Surely Hagar faced the same confusion, sadness, and despair. The loneliness, abandonment, and hopelessness. I wept as I read how, like me, she cried out to God. And he heard her misery.

He even pursued her and told her, in effect, that she wasn't a useless piece of trash. She was part of his plan. God himself gave her baby a name, and Hagar the Egyptian slave saw God face to face. Now that is a beautiful thing. And when things got rough for Hagar again, God remained faithful. She and her child were sent away from their home to wander in the desert with nothing but a sack of food and a little water. When the water ran dry and death was inevitable, she couldn't bare the pain of watching her son die, so she placed her child under a bush. As she walked away, the Scriptures say that she sobbed.

When I had to flee to the safe house, I thought I had lost my sons, and nothing I had experienced thus far in my trial had ever come close to that pain. So I couldn't imagine how excruciating that moment was for Hagar. The text doesn't say that Hagar prayed to God and told him her son was crying. It says that the crying of that child reached the ears of the Creator, and he was moved with compassion. Hagar may have lacked the strength to pray, but God was God. And here's the kicker. All along, there had been a well full of water right in front of Hagar. But God didn't open her eyes to see it until she had reached the end of herself. When she gave up, God moved. And the story didn't end there. "Lift the boy up and take him by the hand, for I will make him into a great nation" (Genesis 21:18). God can make anything beautiful.

This is what we can learn from Hagar.

The Gap-Toothed Saint

When I was ten or so, we lived down the street from a sleazy motel, which was the local meet-up spot for hookers and their customers. Outside the motel were newspaper racks full of pornography. Child pornography, to be exact. I would march my freckle-faced, gap-toothed self down that busy urban thoroughfare all by myself, wrapping paper and scotch tape in hand. And I'd cover those hideous pictures. Until someone decided to expose the filth again.

The Lord brought this memory before me at the one-year mark after Chad's death threat. Our whole church was fasting, and I'd decided to give it my all. My counselor gently suggested I lean into a new direction, one that did not come easy to me. I was to stop trying so hard, to remember that God accepted me just as I was. Three days into the water-and-juice only phase, I was a pile of mush on the floor, overwhelmed with self-criticism. Once I stopped thinking about myself and started listening to the Spirit, I discerned why I was still carrying such negativity after giving my testimony. It was because, for the first time in my adult life, I told the truth about myself. I still felt naked and vulnerable at the memory of it, as if I had betrayed myself, giving everyone a glimpse of the me I didn't want to be. The fearful, shameful, failure that was me.

When I asked the Lord to reveal why I was so beaten down, he brought me face to face with that freckle-faced child who was also me. I saw her repeatedly making that trek down to the sleazy motel on my mission to stop evil, if only for a little while. I heard the Lord's reassuring voice. *That blessed my heart when you did that, Jenny. You didn't do it to earn my approval. You did it because you have a heart for exploited children, and you love righteousness. Not everything you have done in your life has been to earn my approval or the approval of others. Just rest in who I am. Just be who I made you.*

Not two weeks ago, I had looked a drug addict in the face and told her, "God loves you when you are getting high just as much as he does when you sober and going to church. God's love for you doesn't change based on your behavior." I believed that.

I had been naked and vulnerable before God my entire life, and he totally accepted me every single time.

Later that night I decided to enter into the next phase of the fast, so I fixed myself a vegan snack and imagined myself as that little girl. I saw myself sitting on a swing in the local park, eating my snack and laughing with Jesus. Being myself. Feeling comfortable and accepted. I no longer felt uncomfortable about my testimony. This was who I was. Now was the time for the real me to stand up. All the good, the bad, and everything in between. I ended the night by doing something I had been resisting. I had recently read *The Furious Longing of God* by Brennan Manning, in which he suggests meditatively speaking over and over again the phrase "Abba, I belong to you."[1]

I had given it a go before. But I decided tonight I would really open my heart to the Father's healing. I set my timer for twenty minutes and began. By the third "Abba," alligator tears streamed down my cheeks. After twenty minutes I felt like a new person. No more torturous thoughts about my worth. No wondering if I was righteous enough for God to save me. I was loved and accepted because God is love.

In the weeks that followed, God revealed to me that my life story was relevant to all sorts of people. My testimony was not about escaping abuse. It was about escaping bondage. Even though I had belonged to Christ since childhood, I had been walking around for most of my life bound with invisible chains. With every painful childhood experience, the powers of darkness placed chains of unworthiness, abandonment, and inadequacy on my little body and soul. And during my marriage, the chains of fear and shame were added.

Christ came to set the captives free, but not only free from sin and death. He came to free us from our chains of bondage. He came to release us to do even greater things than he did (see John 14:12).

I couldn't possibly be the only person who was walking around in chains of bondage. Perhaps by hearing my story, others would find courage to allow Jesus to bust them loose. Just as he had for me.

17

THE SWORD OF THE SPIRIT

No wonder the Apostle Paul likened the Word of God to a sword. It had become my offensive weapon of warfare.

When my crisis began I was very intentional in how I read the Bible. I didn't flip around haphazardly. I followed a Bible-reading plan that took me simultaneously through both the Old and New Testaments from beginning to end. Without fail, the circumstances unfolding in the Scriptures applied directly to whatever I was experiencing at the time.

It was no coincidence that when I was filled with terror and struggling with hopelessness and dread, I was reading the book of Isaiah, the prophet whose name means, "The Lord saves." The pages brimmed with encouragement to rely on God for rescue because he desires to release his people from oppression, and only he is mighty to save. It overflows with prophecies pointing to Jesus, who would usher in peace and safety.

Not by chance, when my soul needed healing, I arrived at the Gospels, where I read about Jesus loving people back to wholeness. And when my trial was most severe, I happened to be reading the words of the Apostle Paul, a man who endured beatings, shipwrecks, jail, and a mysterious "thorn in his flesh" with patient endurance. I was encouraged to overcome and finish strong.

And just when I was questioning my life's path, wondering why God was allowing me to endure so much suffering, I read about Jacob's son

Joseph and was encouraged to trust in God's plan even when I couldn't see the end. I recognized, when I read his story, that even as Joseph was being restored to his family, even when God was turning things around and finally fulfilling his promises, there were still losses and gut-wrenching tears. "And he wept so loudly that the Egyptians heard him, and Pharaoh's household heard about it" (Genesis 45:2). I know what this kind of crying is all about and it's better described as wailing. And it really hurts. Yet God is still God, and he is still good.

This is what we can learn from Joseph.

Be Strong and Courageous

While I was reading about all the signs and wonders the Lord performed before Pharaoh so that his people could be set free, God was performing signs and wonders on my behalf. And like the Israelites I often looked back toward my place of captivity and questioned the goodness of God. I grumbled about my circumstances, as had they, yet God in his great mercy just kept loving me and leading me.

And when I was self-focused and going crazy with thoughts of my worth, asking, *Am I righteous enough for God to see this victory through?* I had received an answer straight from Deuteronomy that blew my mind and set my heart at ease.

> After the Lord your God has driven them out before you, do not say to yourself, "The Lord has brought me here to take possession of this land because of my righteousness." No, it is on account of the wickedness of these nations that the Lord is going to drive them out before you. It is not because of your righteousness or integrity that you are going in to take possession of their land; but on account of the wickedness of these nations, the Lord your God will drive them out before you. (Deuteronomy 9:4–5)

Words cannot adequately describe the peace that enveloped me as I read those words. No more fearing that if I wasn't perfect all the time,

God would take away his blessing and leave me to die. He was going to give me the victory because the abuse of women is wrong. God keeps his promises and destroys wickedness. That is what we can learn from Moses and the Israelites.

And now, as my court date drew near, it wasn't happenstance that I was reading the story of Joshua. If God had brought me to this place a few weeks or even months earlier, I would likely have lowered my head in defeat and waved a white flag. But now I carried the sword of the Spirit.

Like the Israelites when Joshua came on the Bible scene, I stood on a precipice, facing my most intense battle yet. Much testing, trial, and refining, through which God's faithfulness had been revealed along with many wonders, was behind me.

Similarly, the nation of Israel had been freed from captivity in Egypt and was on the brink of entering the promised land. But when Moses sent Joshua and some other men to scout out the land, they returned with reports of powerful people and fortified cities. "There is absolutely no way we can win" was the logical conclusion for most of them. They wanted to hightail it back to Egypt.

But Joshua and his companion, Caleb, didn't join in their doomsday predictions. Joshua tried to talk sense into them. "The land we passed through and explored is exceedingly good," he pleaded. "If the Lord is pleased with us, he will lead us into that land, a land flowing with milk and honey. And will give it to us. Only do not rebel against the Lord. Do not be afraid of the people of the land, because we will devour them. Their protection is gone. But the Lord is with us. Do not be afraid of them" (Numbers 14:7–9).

How was Joshua able to display such courage while others melted in fear? How could I march confidently into my own battle when the odds were so against me?

Because of the fears of his doubting fellow countrymen, Joshua was forced to wait out a forty-year detour before entering the land God promised. He kept his focus on his great God instead of his circumstances, remembering everything God had already done for his people. I'm sure

God used that time to further build his faith, so that when it came time to do battle, Joshua was ready.

As I wrote this chapter, I was tucked safely in bed, completely free from terror and oppression. That was a miracle. One of my sons relaxed happily beside me, watching television and asking me for a back-scratch. This too was a miracle. Despite working no overtime this month, I was current on all my bills. And God had broken my chains of shame, pride, and unworthiness. Miracles, all!

As I surveyed the land God was leading me to, I would choose to be like Joshua. Yes, my enemies were powerful, and there was no reason for my optimism, but I would keep my eyes on God. Nothing was impossible with him.

The woman who made out a will and bought life insurance back when her life was threatened had not been a woman ready for this battle. Every difficult thing God had allowed up to this point was going to serve me well. From this precipice, I could see the spirits of fear forming ranks, readying to prey on my old vulnerabilities. The spirits of pride were sharpening their weapons, confident I could be enticed to allow them to regain dominion over me. The spirits of shame were preparing their arrows of accusation. The lying spirits were marching into formation, preparing to assault the goodness of God and the truth of his love for me. God saw all of this. And he was calling me, his child, to face them in battle.

He only asked one thing of me. He was calling me to stand. Stand on his promises. On his goodness. On his faithfulness. On his word. And in my spirit I hear his directive. *Have I not commanded you, Jenny? Be strong and courageous. Do not be afraid. Do not be discouraged, for the Lord your God will be with you wherever you go* (see Joshua 1:9).

The battle belongs to the Lord. This is what we can learn from Joshua.

18

PLUNDER FROM THE FIERCE

*I*n a cozy booth at Outback Steakhouse, Maria began to share her story. A beautiful and fiery Latina in her seventies, Maria recalled her long-ago triumph over spousal abuse. Of living a secret life because she was a devout Catholic. Separating from a husband for any reason back then, and especially in the eyes of the church, was immoral. But against all odds, she had survived. Maria had recognized, in her spirit, that the church was wrong. Although pregnant with her third child at the time, she trusted in God and in his love enough to do some really gutsy things to change her life and the lives of her two children.

The consequences of her bravery meant going to the hospital alone to deliver her baby. But she wasn't alone. God took care of her, providing a job that payed wages equal to a man's, unthinkable at that time, and eventually making a way for her to buy her own home. He brought a good man into her life, who adopted her three babies and gave her three more. A man with whom she shared a life of love for forty-nine years, until his recent passing.

Her story had been prompted by my brief mention that I was writing a book. She had asked me what my book was about, and I'd shared my testimony. My new friend, Maria, and I also shared the booth with an old friend with whom I had long been looking forward to catching up. Now this friend took a turn, and what she shared blew my mind.

"I have a testimony that is very much like yours, Jenny, but also very different," she said. She too had been living a secret life. Like me, she had been wounded deeply in childhood. Like me, she'd felt unworthy of God's love and this false belief led her down a path of shame and hiding. The past year had been the worst of her life, yet also the best, because through the horrific pain of facing the truth, God had remade her. He'd freed her from the chains of pride, shame, and unworthiness. Sound familiar?

These kinds of ordained moments, along with the sacred hours I spent at my kitchen table reading God's precious Word through healing tears, my fellowship with the beautiful believers who now met at my house every Thursday night for Bible study, the powerful prayer sessions with my pod, and the ministering I received each week through the anointed worship and preaching at my church, all supplied me with faith to believe the impossible.

I would be retrieving plunder from the fierce.

Whenever I was struck with a new flaming arrow, I ended up on the ground. But with each new assault, I spent less and less time there. Recently I had asked my lawyer, "Do you mean to tell me that even if the judge believes my testimony and refuses Chad's request for spousal support, Chad can just keep taking me to court?"

"Yes, he can."

And then it had hit me. Chad once threatened to do four things if I told anyone about the abuse. One, take me down in flames. Nope. He hadn't killed or even maimed me. God hadn't allowed it. Two, ruin everything I love. Nope. Despite Chad's best efforts to destroy my relationship with my sons—the most important things to me on the planet—they had been restored to me and our relationship was thriving. Three, destroy me. Nope. I was thriving.

And fourth, leave me penniless. But while Chad was busily executing these plans, God was blessing my socks off in miraculous ways. My

401(k) had slowly grown and the value had increased tenfold. Coincidence? I didn't think so.

Finally Safe

It was obvious why I had felt physically and emotionally unsafe. Even now, Chad sometimes ripped the chain lock off my door to get into the house when I wasn't home. But why had I never felt safe spiritually?

I was coming to understand that the truth of who God is had been horribly marred by my painful past. While I was singing "Jesus Loves Me" in Sunday school, I was being sexually abused by someone who claimed to be one of Jesus' followers. Satan took that opportunity to lean in close and whisper a lie that made perfect sense to my innocent, four-year-old ears. *If Jesus truly loved you, wouldn't he protect you?* And while I was being taught all about Jehovah and his ability to provide, there wasn't enough food in my house. *You can't really trust God to take care of you,* came the whispers in the darkness.

Now fast-forward through years of neglect and painful experiences to a twenty-year-old bride, returning to her parents' home the day after her wedding to collect a few things before her honeymoon. She finds all of her belongings stuffed into trash bags and sitting on the front porch. I was that bride, and that was my heart being pierced with the enemy's reminder that I did not matter to anyone. The people who were supposed to love and protect me had not. I wasn't worthy of love and protection. Life was not safe. And God wasn't safe either.

He seemed to me angry, unpredictable, and withholding. Had he really cared, wouldn't he have stopped me from marrying an abuser? Still, even though I believed God was difficult to please and fickle, I just knew I would absolutely die without his presence in my life. If the God who died for mankind rejected me despite all my efforts, it would be the end of me—irrefutable proof that I was unlovable, inherently flawed, and just plain worthless. I never verbalized any of this, of course, fearing others' disapproval. Instead I talked on and on about the unconditional love of

God, wanting badly to believe it was a reality, all the while convinced that it wasn't.

And then came the pivotal moment of my life, requiring me to step out in faith and believe that God wasn't lying when he said he was love. And I stepped out of the boat and walked away. From the perceived safety of my false life. From the acceptance of those religious types whom I'd spent so many years trying to impress. From the safety of my deeply ingrained idea that God would admit me into heaven because I was "good." In one gutsy move, I bet the whole enchilada on Jesus. Either he was real or I was going to drown.

Well, guess what happened? The waves were still rolling and the wind still howled, but I was walking on the water. Jesus was real. He bound me up in his loving arms and was healing my broken heart. I was safe with him. Finally safe.

As I waited for my day in court to arrive, I received the strength to look truthfully into the pain of my childhood and make profound connections between the life I was given as a child and the life I'd chosen for myself as an adult. The tears began to wane, understanding gave way to acceptance, and acceptance gave way to thankfulness. My Abba healed me to the point that I could actually look back on my life, thankful not only for my safety but also for the broken road I had traveled.

19

THOUGH WE STUMBLE,
WE WILL NOT FALL

*M*ore time to pray, I thought, when my court date was rescheduled from March to April thanks to Chad's attorney requesting a continuation. I'd simply enjoy God's presence and experience the joy of a life free from abuse and fear. Then I received word that the court "mis-calendared" things. The judge was unavailable on April 15.

But I couldn't help smiling when I saw the new date—May 13. Exactly the one-year anniversary of my stay in the safe house for battered women. What a way to commemorate my exodus out of the darkness and the faithfulness of my good God. I couldn't wait to see what he was going to do next.

I felt the Spirit telling me he was leading me into a time of testing and refining. I was being called to fast and pray like never before. I was to cling to him with everything in me. I would emerge from my time in the wilderness as a victor, full of power and ready for my showdown with evil in court. *Don't drop your shield of faith, Jenny. I will be with you now, just as always. Hold on to your shield of faith.* I confided in Michelle about the Spirit's directive. She mobilized my pod for a prayer covering.

But less than a week into my time of testing, I'd become consumed by fear, doubts about God's love for me, and dread when I looked ahead to my upcoming trial. The enemy's badgering was relentless!

Recently, my sister had told me about a young woman in terrible circumstances. The Lord brought her to me in my dreams all that night. The next morning, he hounded me until I called her, despite my worry she might think me weird, and despite Satan whispering that it wasn't my business. Our meeting was totally anointed and resulted in a flat-out miracle and victory on behalf of her and her son. When I heard the news, my faith was bolstered.

But I barely had time to rejoice before the accuser started in. *He worked a miracle for her, but he is not going to do the same for you.* Ouch. And the taunts continued. *You are utterly alone. You don't have a special someone. Your sister moved all the way across the country. Your friends have their own families. Your kids are blinded by what Chad is telling them about you.*

What a jerk. Immediately after this particular assault, I got a text from Michelle. Pastor Blaine, who had been so instrumental in my exodus out of the darkness, had called her. I hadn't seen him for a couple of months and now the Spirit had placed me heavily on his heart. Guess what message was given to him by the Spirit? *Jenny needs covering. Don't forget about Jenny.* I wasn't alone after all! I won in that moment, but the onslaught continued. The next morning during my prayer time I was doing my best to fight the lies with truths from God's Word, and to will myself to feel better and be stronger. Unknowingly, I had returned to my former striving, and it was wearing me out and proving ineffective. How would I survive another three-and-a-half weeks like this?

That was when a still, small voice brought calm to the storm raging in my soul. *Just rest under the shadow of my wings. The battle belongs to me. I've got you covered.* I pictured myself nestled against a breast-full of comforting feathers near the heartbeat of God, a majestic wing engulfing my body. Curled up in a little ball, resting securely in the shadow of my great, loving God. The purpose of this time of testing was not to teach me how strong I was or force me to try harder. It was meant to get this very important truth through my thick skull once and for all: No matter how terrifying my circumstances, God was in control. He had me.

Arise

Mother's Day arrived. *What a difference a year made*, I reflected as I picked up my sons. Seth had bought me a pretty yellow orchid and some dark chocolate with his own money. Micah gave me a homemade card. After a fun day together at the beach, I broke my fast—pasta with meat sauce, Italian soda, ice cream. I went all out, and it was delicious!

I slept peacefully, and suddenly my day of destiny was upon me. As soon as the alarm went off, the following passage of Scripture came to me: "Arise my darling, my beautiful one, come with me. See! The winter is past; the rains are over and gone. Flowers appear on the earth; the season of singing has come, the cooing of the doves is heard in our land. The fig tree forms it early fruit; the blossoming vines spread their fragrance. Arise, come, my darling; my beautiful one, come with me" (Song of Songs 2:10–13).

Thanks to author Brennan Manning, I had meditated on this passage and understood that the words were from Jesus to his beloved—namely, us.[1] I spent two hours with Jesus at the kitchen table, reviewing all the things he had done for me and in me, telling him I was completely surrendered to the will of the Father because God knew best. I also thanked him for refining me in the furnace of affliction. What a dummy! Maybe I was getting a little too spiritual for my own good!

When my friends came to pick me up for court, I felt nothing but peace. No nervous energy. No anxiety. Just the peace that passes understanding.

Just Keep Rowing

I had told everyone that after my trial I was going to have a banana split. Only now I didn't feel like eating ever again.

But a sweet friend texted me to say it was time to go out and get that banana split and we should bring our kids along. So I pulled myself together and left my bedroom pity-party-for-one behind. Head aching and heavyhearted, I drove the boys to the local Dairy Queen. *This was supposed to be the banana split of victory,* I thought to myself as I examined the frozen treat.

My big day in court hadn't turned out the way I believed it would. What about the promise that I would overcome by the blood of the Lamb and the word of my testimony? I hadn't even got to testify! Why had God turned a blind eye? Where was my justice? It wasn't allowed because there had never been a domestic violence conviction against Chad. Apparently, escaping an abusive situation before serious harm or death does not help one in a court of law. The judge had punched some numbers into his computer and ordered me to pay not only child support but monthly spousal support as well. And if that wasn't enough, Chad's attorney requested the payments be retroactive. With a swipe of a pen, I was already five thousand dollars in the hole. Even worse, there was no way I could afford to pay spousal support and keep the home. I would have to sell it, and the boys and I would be forced to move into a rental.

And then it had been over. Stunned, I exited the courtroom with my bewildered friends and devastated attorney. That was when Barb approached me. Before the trial began, I'd seen her enter the courtroom and take a seat in a back row. It wrecked me that she had come to testify on Chad's behalf. But the Spirit spoke up. *Tell her that you love her.* I tried to ignore that little message, but it came again. Truth be told, I did love her very much, but was now the time to say it? I turned around, and our eyes met.

"I just want you to know that I love you very much," I said.

Barb smiled back and told me she loved me too, as she pulled a paper out of her purse. "I got a subpoena," she said.

As I left the courtroom, defeated, Barb explained that the only reason she came was because she had been served a subpoena and was only going to answer questions about what she saw the night before I went to the shelter. If she had been called to testify, it would have backfired on Chad and actually helped my case.

"But it is so unfair!" I cried. "It's so unjust that I have to pay him just so I can keep breathing!" Barb's response let me know that perhaps she was beginning to see things more clearly than I had thought.

"I know it is, but now you are free. I am letting him vent to me to keep things calm for you. I'm keeping him out of your house, so you can be free."

Barb was right. I realized she had been spending considerable time and effort working behind the scenes to keep me safe and Chad calm. She had sacrificed much for me, but I had been unable to see it. I was so thankful that I listened to the Spirit's direction to express my love for her. If I had been disobedient, I might not have learned the truth, and it would have left an open door to bitterness.

I took a deep breath and decided to eat that banana split in faith. With each delicious bite, I swallowed down anger, disappointment, self-pity, disillusionment, pride, desire for vengeance, confusion, unbelief, and despair. Twenty minutes later, the bowl was empty and my heart was lighter. I was so thankful that my Abba knew I was only dust, and I asked him to forgive me for accusing him of all the wrong things. I so wanted to lay down in the soft sand of my new shore and finally give my blistered hands a break, but I was just going to have to keep rowing. To feel the tension release from every one of my sore muscles, while I sat up in the sand and gazed with amazement at the raging sea that I had successfully crossed. But it just wasn't time.

And that is when Jesus reminded me that I hadn't been rowing alone. I had only come as far as I had because he was with me.

Whenever we decide to allow him to, he'll take over the oars for the rest of the journey.

So I moved over, and he climbed in and took a seat on the bench beside me. I saw his smile as he gripped the oars with tender, nail-scarred hands, prompting me to rest my hands on his. Together we started rowing.

20

A New Perspective

The key to overcoming disaster and disappointment, I was learning, was remaining open to the leading of the Spirit.

A week had passed since my day in court, and already I no longer viewed it as a defeat. Every promise God had made to me was fulfilled in some way on May 13. And their more complete fulfillment was yet to come. God knew me better than I knew myself, of course, and if the day had gone the way I thought it should, pride would have been difficult to resist. In my spirit I would secretly have been saying, "Attention, all! I am the champion of the world! God is really with me, and now everyone knows it! All my fasting, praying, and faith led to this mighty victory!" I could just imagine Master Yoda looking at me in awe and saying, "The force is strong with this one, yes."

In reading *Abba's Child* by Brennan Manning in recent months, I'd came face to face with my "impostor," or false self.[1] My impostor was birthed through childhood abandonment and rejection, and she had been an important part of my childhood survival. But when I became an adult, my impostor stunted my growth as a whole, healthy person, she fostered my preoccupation with the approval of others, and she blinded me to the truth about my identity in Jesus. In recent months I had acknowledged my impostor, thanked her for helping me to get through a difficult childhood, and told her it was time now for her to leave.

Although she had exited the house, she still hung out on the front porch, waiting to slip back in. And if I had walked away with this final victory having gone down just the way I had planned it, the strength of my impostor would have most certainly increased.

On the other hand, having to tell my family and friends that the day in court, over which I had been proclaiming certain victory, had ended in epic defeat was very good for growth of my true self. It kept me grounded, and gave others a chance to amaze me with their capacity for compassion, empathy, and love. I was forced to humble myself under God's mighty hand, so he could lift me up in due time. Enduring Chad's gloating certainly kept pride at bay.

Maintaining the peace I'd found while eating my banana split of faith would be difficult.

A Bitter Root

"Don't let him get to you. You are almost there," Leslie said, when we discussed some new ways Chad was trying to exert control. "He's losing his grip on you and so he is trying to rattle you." She was right, and her words should have brought peace, but my emotional fog was still present and intensifying.

It was Pentecost Sunday, and I drove to church that evening with a heavy heart, after what should have been a fine day—time with my sons, surfing with friends, lunch at In-N-Out Burger. I sat through the worship, feeling like the dry bones God told Ezekiel to prophesy to. I lifted my hands but felt nothing. Why wasn't God answering my call for a fresh anointing? His answer hit me like a punch in the gut. I was overwhelmed with bitterness, hatred, and unforgiveness.

It had been relatively easy to escape all these traps of Satan when I was experiencing victory at every turn. Not so easy when I was the one being crushed and taunted. *You are falling prey to the very same things that are destroying Chad.* The pastor invited to the altar all who needed a "mighty rushing wind of the Spirit" to blow the pollution out of their lives. Tears streaming, I hightailed it to the front row. *I can't do this alone, Jesus. Please help me. I don't want to be bitter. I don't want to nurse hatred. I choose to forgive Chad. Help me forgive Chad.*

Literally in one moment, the beautiful rushing wind took it all away on that Pentecost Sunday. I was delivered from the dark toxic cloud of bitterness, hatred, and unforgiveness that had created a fog-like barrier between me and my precious Lord. Thanks be to God.

> *Journal Entry:*
>
> *I'm waiting for Chad's attorney to send a written agreement so that I can put the house on the market, because Chad is refusing to cooperate without one. I am going to sell my home and all my furniture and start over. Although the thought of starting from scratch is daunting, I am filled with nervous excitement because I know God is for me and not against me. I know the rest of my life is going to be the best of my life. I just have to keep rowing toward the shore. Following the little bit of light he gives me each day.*

Friends, there is absolutely no way, in these kinds of circumstances, we could be freed from these pains had not Father God sent his Spirit to help us. Jesus said we would receive power when the Holy Ghost came upon us, which happens the moment we choose to turn to him in repentance and surrender our hearts and lives to him. We receive the power to forgive, even when there has been no apology. We have the power to bless those who persecute us, as Jesus did.

I Say Yes

In truth, many times I fantasized about Chad being struck by a massive bolt of lightning. *May the skies open up and heaven proclaim judgment upon him!* Although I'd been freed from the poison of bitterness, I had to keep saying no to anger and unforgiveness on nearly a daily basis. This was the truth of where I was at.

Every time Chad slammed a door in my face or sent a text rant, I'd feel my flesh prickling, and I'd have to re-confess. But I refused to succumb to Satan's ploy. I could choose to obey Jesus and bless those who persecuted me. I could even pray for my enemies, for the sake of my own healing.

Journal Entry:

Through the power of the Holy Spirit, I now view Chad as an instrument of my refining. Satan wants to use Chad's behavior to lure me into anger, thereby opening a door to his evil work in my life and giving him an opportunity to destroy me. Instead, I am going to use all the conflict as an opportunity to be refined by God. This plan is working.

The good news is that there is nothing left to argue over or dispute in court. No matter how long Chad delays the selling of the home and the finalizing of the divorce, it is essentially done. I can move forward in confidence and just live my life, knowing God has everything under control.

When I began my journey out of the darkness, I often told myself it was so Chad might have a fighting chance at victory over his sin that I was making my stand. At this point, I was no longer certain that his victory was ever a true motive. Perhaps I had needed to tell myself that, so I could feel better about my decision. Now that I was stronger and my impostor was in check, I no longer needed to make up religious-sounding reasons for breaking free.

I'd made the right decision because I was never meant to be abused or killed.

Eighteen months ago I'd written, "I literally have no idea in what way my salvation is coming, but I know with absolute certainty that it is."

Today I was alive, unbound, and unharmed. My trials weren't over, but I had been saved from much. And now God's newly freed child was ready to live the rest of her life for him.

Lord, I choose to say yes. Yes to every request for prayer and every invitation to speak healing into a broken life. Yes to every opportunity to listen to someone who just needs to talk and every chance to break bread with a friend, new or old. Yes to every open door and every spiritual battle. I just say yes.

21

GLORIA DIOS!

At 10:30 p.m., I received a text message that started my heart racing and got me out of bed. A dear friend was outside my home, and she needed a place to stay. I opened the door to find a woman who looked much like I had when I fled to my friend Steph's house in the middle of the night—bewildered, terrified, and lost. Her abusive husband had kicked her out of the house, and it wasn't safe for her to return. We had been praying God would give her discernment about whether or not she should physically leave her abusive situation, and God was now answering. But that didn't make her pain any less real as she stood in my living room, trying to make sense of what had just happened.

Like me, her children were staying with her abuser. Like me, she had nothing to her name but what she quickly shoved into a small bag. She hadn't eaten or slept. Her face was stained with tears. We said a prayer together, and I tucked her into the guest bedroom just as Steph had done for me.

After she made it through that long, dark night, God started proving just how powerful he was. Each day we went to battle, praying the Holy Spirit would move in the heart of her eldest son. In the past, he had stepped up many times to protect and defend her, and I felt strongly in my spirit that his support was crucial to her victory. A few days later, he told her that he would indeed stay by her side, and the two of them decided to look for an apartment together.

The next miracle she needed was to find an apartment in the area, which was hard to come by. A week or so later, her husband relayed through her son that she must return "his" car and cell phone. Because I was now acquainted with the legal system, I informed her that what was his was hers and vice versa. The car he currently drove belonged to her as much as it belonged to him, and the car she currently drove belonged to both of them as well. "How will you get your younger son to and from school without a car?" I asked her. "And how will you get to work?"

I recognized the battered-woman response: take the path of least resistance. I let her know she wasn't going to respond like that anymore. And then we went to war, rebuking the enemy, commanding any demons to back off in the name of Jesus. There was no further mention of the car or the phone.

While we waited for God to provide an apartment, we sang praise songs in the evenings as she played the piano. The Lord continued to deliver her from fear and shame with each passing day. Like me, these chains had been placed on her little body when she was very young. She endured the pain of severe, prolonged sexual abuse as a child, which Satan used to lead her down a dark path. Like me, she had been married for over two decades and her abuse had started immediately. Like me, she chose to stay. Like me, she lived a lie, working tirelessly to make everyone believe she had a wonderful marriage.

Publicly she served the Lord through her music ministry. Meanwhile, she was completely consumed with darkness. An affair led to an unwanted pregnancy and a secret abortion. She continued singing in church and keeping her secrets until Jesus messed it all up.

Like he had with me, he'd sought her out and told her it was time. Time to face her truth. Time to confess her part in everything. Time to trust him with the results. Despite suicidal thoughts and horrible despair, she obeyed, confessing everything to her husband and her older children.

That is when everything appeared to start unraveling. Despite the fact that her husband was also unfaithful during the marriage, he refused to forgive her and his violent rage only intensified.

But Jesus.

Jesus said it's the truth that sets us free. My friend's obedience to Jesus became the first step toward freedom from abuse. Two weeks later, there was only one thing holding her back. She hadn't told her mother or siblings, and despite their earlier support when she'd been beaten, Satan was doing a good job convincing my friend that her family wouldn't be able to forgive her if they knew everything. But she stepped out in faith and confessed and received both acceptance and forgiveness.

On a Sunday while I was at work, I noticed a text from my friend. Two big things had happened—one bad and one good. Her eldest son was backing out and had decided to stay with his dad. And the landlord of a beautiful two-bedroom apartment right up the road—the one she wanted the most—had offered the rental to her.

"Oh hey, I was just looking for you. I'm going to send you home," said my supervisor.

I just about passed out. I'd been praying for this day off. When I got home, my friend and I sang praises and prayed. Then she called the landlord, who offered to meet her right away to sign paperwork and be given the keys. Stunned, my friend told her she was planning to go to church that evening and asked if we could stop by afterward. The landlord readily agreed, and we soon discovered that she lived less than three miles from the church!

Next we prayed the Holy Spirit would move in her eldest son's heart, and we took dominion over the dark forces attempting to interfere with her son's loyalty. She called him on the way to church. Victory! Her son agreed to share the new rental and reaffirmed his support for her.

"I was overwhelmed with applications for this apartment," the landlord said to my friend as she escorted us to the dining table in her exquisite home. "But I was so impressed with you, and I am pleased to offer the apartment to you and your son."

My friend's beaming smile faded into a look of concern. "I just have a question. About the money, how much do I need to pay today?" The entire sum required was about three thousand dollars. My friend did not have anywhere near this amount, nor could she pay me back for a loan this size. But the Spirit was tapping me on the shoulder. *Hey there, remember all those years you neglected to tithe? I have made it possible for you to act in this moment. You are going to make a good profit when you sell your home. Trust me.*

"I know," I said casually. "I have my checkbook with me and I can just write a check for the amount, and you can give me the money when we get home." My friend looked confused. Her expression said, "Are you crazy?" But I just winked and smiled. Let's reflect, shall we? Two years ago I was working two jobs, was overloaded with debt and at risk of losing my house. Presently, with no doing of my own, I was working only one full-time job, was current on all my bills, and had the ability to write out a large check. God had given my friend favor with her new landlord, who just happened to be a successful Christian woman, and was providing the necessary funds through an overflow of blessing to me.

If I had the money in my possession, I explained to my friend as we drove away, and did not respond to the Spirit's directive in that moment, I would have been disobedient. And as usual, the miracles didn't end there. She brought both of her sons to the beautiful apartment on the following day, and they were thrilled. As they toured the grounds, the boys discovered that the worship leader at their church lived next door!

At last the moment came for her to tell her husband that she had secured an apartment. When she told him that God was working on her behalf, his rage intensified and he went straight for his secret weapon. "So does your family know about all the things you have done?"

"Yes," she replied with the confidence and strength that comes from being completely cleansed by the blood of the Lamb. "I told them everything, and they forgive me." His attitude changed abruptly. (I could imagine the demons in that moment, writhing in agony as she crushed the darkness with the light of the truth.) He lowered his head and allowed her to take anything she wanted.

The next day my friend called her mother in Mexico to tell her the good news. Hearing that God had moved in a miraculous fashion, and that her daughter was finally going to be free, she exclaimed, "Gloria Dios! Gloria Dios!" *Glory to God! Glory to God!*

This was the point of my entire story to date. Even though I was still walking through my own fiery trial, the Lord had brought me to a place where I was already able to reach out to others. My new policy as a "yes woman" was leading to all sorts of amazing experiences and a fuller, richer life.

Glory to God indeed.

22

A Place for Us

They say you don't realize Jesus is all you need until Jesus is all you have.

On a gray November morning two years prior, my sister backed out of the driveway, waved goodbye, and moved across the country. I stood on my patio choking back tears and watched until her car was no longer in view, knowing my tiny shred of security drove away with her. At the time, Holly was my very last hope in this world, the only one with any understanding of the life I was living. I felt that without her I had absolutely nothing. I would be utterly alone.

But that was exactly what needed to happen. When Holly left, I had no one except Jesus. I barely knew him at the time, but I have since learned that he is absolutely enough. I am his and he is mine. He is real and he does what he said he came to do.

I thought about this as I emptied out the garage, preparing for an open house, which was on hold until I received the go-ahead to sell. The boys were cleaning their rooms as well. Next I tackled the junk drawer in the kitchen, feeling secure in the knowledge that I was Jesus' and he was mine. I sorted through all my clothes and staged a bunch of stuff for donation to Goodwill. Lastly, I planted annuals in the clay pots on the front patio.

Journal Entry:

Lord, there is still one huge prayer yet unanswered, and it's a doozy. I need to a place for the boys and I to live. A "double portion for my shame," something I can afford. I asked the boys what was important to them besides staying close to their school, and my heart sank. It's clear they both really want to live in a house. Not a townhouse or a condo—a house. It could be small, and it doesn't have to be fancy. Seth says he doesn't care if it's the size of a cardboard box as long as we get a better internet provider. Micah wants to be able to ride his skateboard in a cul-de-sac and shoot hoops in the front yard. He'd also like a garage, where his friends can come play pool and listen to music. I know you're big enough to provide a house with good internet, a garage for the drums, and even room for my doggies.

For several months I had been fantasizing about living in the brand-new, glittery and glamorous housing development down the road. I even toured the model homes. A two-bedroom would do just fine, thank you very much. But the more I prayed about it, the more I began to feel a heaviness in my spirit asking for a fancy bungalow. I sensed I wasn't praying in accordance with God's will.

Were my motives for wanting to move into the fancy new development based totally in the flesh? I couldn't deny that part of my dream of living in such an elegant development was that Chad would have to drive up to an exclusive gated community when he picked up the kids. Each time he drove past the well-manicured lawns, elegant lighting fixtures, and the rows of Queen Anne palms, I would be sticking it to him for being such a jerk.

I perused the internet every night for rental properties, but the results were discouraging. Then I got a text from my friend Cindy—a photo of a house with a for-lease sign in front of it, along with the message, "In my neighborhood. FYI." I drove by the tract and really liked it. Bummer—it was out of my price range. Not to mention that I still didn't have a signed divorce judgment and couldn't put my house on the market until that happened. I decided to put it out of my mind. But when my head hit the pillow each night I dreamed of the little tract house across the street from Cindy. And I started praying differently.

The house looked small from the outside, and it wasn't new or fancy. But something about it made me feel like it could be a home for me and my boys. A few days later, I made an appointment to see the house. I put my hair up in a professional-looking bun and wore my only pair of dress slacks. *Dear Lord,* I prayed, heading out the door, *if this is of you, please give me favor with the owner.*

A cherry-red Lexus pulled into the driveway just as I arrived, and a robust, distinguished-looking gentleman with olive skin, a gray goatee, and a snazzy cap got out. "Hello, Jenny. My name is Mike. It is very nice to meet you." His accent matched the one that had met my ears during our telephone conversation. Mike was both warm and professional.

Crossing the threshold, I realized the house was much more spacious than I had originally thought. It even had a beautiful family room with a fireplace. I tried to appear calm, but my heart beat faster and faster with every step. "This is the courtyard," Mike said. I visualized how lovely the space would look with my many potted succulents, hibiscus plants, hydrangeas, and hanging baskets scattered about in all the right places.

The house wasn't showy, but it was perfect for my sons. It was close to a park, their school, their church, and their dad's house. It was even on a cul-de-sac and had a garage big enough for a set of drums and a pool table. Pets were allowed, and our basketball hoop would fit right in.

"Do you like it?" Mike asked as we made our way into the kitchen.

"I do. It is a beautiful home." I took a deep breath and explained my whole situation. "I'd be willing to sign a two-year lease in order to get reduced rent. I understand that this house will most likely be leased tomorrow, but if it happens to still be available when I put my home on the market, I hope you will consider me." My heart was thumping away, and I hoped my cheeks weren't as flushed as they felt.

Mike looked both puzzled and pleased. "I appreciate you being honest with me about your situation. I also went through a long and difficult divorce, and I know how tough that is. I am the property manager, not the owner, by the way." He told me to keep in touch.

Nothing about the tract house would feed my vain conceit, I thought as I drove away. *Abba, you know exactly how to bless me without feeding my flesh. It would take a flat-out miracle for this home to still be available when I am ready, but I want you to know that I would love to live here. This house would definitely be a double portion for my shame.*

When Michelle and I were surfing a week or so later, she suggested I pray and "march" around the property seven times—just like Joshua had when he needed God to bring down the walls of Jericho. Cindy eagerly agreed to join me, along with her adorable preschooler, John. We quickly decided we couldn't very well walk around the actual house without being arrested for trespassing (and looking like complete lunatics to my potential future neighbors). So we all mounted our bikes. Little John eagerly snapped his helmet strap. His little legs pumped furiously. "What are we doing?" he asked.

"We're going to ride around the neighborhood seven times and pray that Jenny can rent a house nearby," his mom answered.

"Ooh, Jenny is going to be our neighbor?"

"That's what we are praying for."

"Seven times?"

"Yep."

"Why?"

"Because that's what Joshua did when he needed a miracle."

"Oh. Are we going to get tired?"

"Probably."

As we approached the house for the first time, I reached my hand toward it. "Dear Jesus, if it is your will, I ask that the boys and I can move into this house. Amen." Each time we came back around to the house, one of us added a new prayer.

"How many left?" John asked, his cheeks pink.

"Four," I said. "Hey, buddy, thanks so much for helping, but it's okay if you need to rest."

He looked at me with his big brown eyes. "No. I will keep helping you." Pretty soon though, we talked him into taking a break with a neighbor. Cindy and I continued to pedal until we had reached our goal of encircling the house seven times. When we finished, I was sweaty and thirsty, but my heart felt light. And I was so grateful for the blessing of good friends.

Something Is Happening

"God will save your children. They will be blessed because you are leaving a legacy of faith."

I'd approached the altar after Sunday evening service to receive a blessing and was given this word from the Lord. But now discouragement stalked me. When I returned home and went upstairs to check on the boys, everything had gone to hell in a handbasket.

Seth wore a hopelessness in his eyes that reminded me of how I used to look like when I was the one bearing the brunt of Chad's criticism. "What's going on?" I asked.

"When Dad sits me down and tells me that I am a disappointment, an utter failure, and basically the lowest thing on the planet, it makes me want to not care about anything." Tears welled up in my eyes and I stood up.

"None of those things are true about you, honey," I said, tears pressing behind my eyes. "Please believe me. Your dad is not well. He should be taking his medicine and he isn't."

Meanwhile, Micah stormed into his room. I found him lying on his bed crying. I approached the bed and sat down. "Honey, I know you're angry with me for getting a divorce." I waited until he was ready to respond.

"Yeah, I am pretty angry all right!" All his pent-up emotion finally spilled out.

"I am so sorry. I know you don't understand, and if there were any other way, I would have chosen it. But I had no choice." Now both of us were sobbing.

"But the Bible says that you can never get a divorce under any circumstances!" I couldn't believe I was hearing this from my fourteen-year-old. Clearly Chad was filling him with all sorts of propaganda.

"That is not true." I went to the Scriptures and explained divorce from both Old and New Testament perspectives. "There are valid reasons for divorce because people sin against each other. God doesn't want married couples to dump each other when life gets hard or to trade in their spouse for a new model when marriage gets tough. I'm not doing either of those things. I am sorry, but I had to get a divorce."

"But why?"

I rubbed my temples and searched for the right words. "You are young, sweetheart, and so there are things that I can't tell you."

"But that's just it! I want to know why!"

I prayed silently for wisdom. "There are things a husband is not allowed to do to a wife. Your dad has been doing these things to me since before you were born."

He stopped crying and looked at me with interest. "Since before I was born?"

"Yes, honey. I prayed for twenty-two years for it to stop, and when it didn't stop, I got really mad at God and blamed him. And then I realized it isn't God's fault. We all have a free will, and your dad refused to stop doing the things that were wrong. And then something really bad happened. Something so bad that I believe that if I didn't get a divorce, I might not still be here." My son was hanging on every word. "I hate seeing you going back and forth between two homes and feeling so much pain. But you need to trust me. Have I ever done anything that wasn't good for you and your brother?"

"No."

"Then I have to ask you to trust me. But I am so sorry."

We stood in his room, squeezing each other tightly for a long, long time. I went into Seth's room and asked him why he was blaring his music so loud. "I was just angry about Dad, but I'm better now." He turned the music down low. And then it was all over.

But seeing my kids suffer this way was costing me much. Even after crying through the night, my grief followed me into the next day. I held it together while dropping the boys off at school, then loaded my surfboard into the car. I sobbed all the way to the beach and while I paddled through a pounding surf. As I peeled off my wetsuit, I listened to a new voicemail. "Jen, this is Cindy. I talked to Mike. He said he liked you the moment that he met you. He really wants to rent to you, but you need to act. You have to fill out an application."

I love you, Jesus. I know you are with me. Please show me if this is from you. I need you to make it clear. My crying ordeal over, I did the laundry, bought some groceries, and watered the lawn. Before long, it was time to meet up with Mike. Cindy and another girlfriend, Angela, walked with me to the rental, along with little John. No way was Mike going to able to resist that smile and those cheeks and the mop of brown curls crowning John's head. While the ladies toured the house, Mike directed me to the kitchen. His casual demeanor changed in an instant and he became very serious.

"You need to know something," he said. I swallowed the lump in my throat. "Something is happening here." He pointed his index finger to the sky and bounced it up and down. "Someone is helping you. Every day I have qualified people coming over here who are ready to rent this house on the spot for full rent. I keep saying no, because of you, and I don't even know why." He shook his head and shrugged his shoulders. "Never, ever have I reduced the rent, and yet I am willing to do it for you." Even he seemed confused by this strange behavior.

I was fighting back tears. "I know why."

"You do?"

"Yes. It's God's favor. If I end up this in this home, it will be a miracle and an answer to months and months of prayer. No matter what happens, you will be blessed for your kindness to me."

He nodded. "What I really liked is that you were honest with me about your situation. I have a soft spot in my heart for you. Someone put it there. But . . ." Now he leaned toward me and spoke softly. "You need to do your part. I can wait for you until October 15 and not one day more."

If I needed a flashing neon sign that said, "Take a step in faith," I had gotten it.

Mike led me out front. "Let me tell you something else. I wasn't always a Christian. I was raised Muslim. Something in me made me want to convert, and three years ago I did it! I became a Christian!" His countenance was beaming as he spoke of finding Jesus, and together our motley group experienced a holy moment in the driveway. "If you are a Christian, you know the story of Joshua?" I asked.

"Yes, of course!"

I told Mike about how Cindy, John, and I had ridden our bikes around the block seven times. That was just too much for Mike to take. "You must meet my pastor! You must meet my pastor!" he said.

As we waved goodbye, little John trotted in front of us toward Cindy's house. "Is Jenny going to get the house?" he asked.

What a good question. Something was definitely happening here, and now it was time for me to do my part. I just needed to figure out exactly what that meant.

23

AND THE WALLS CAME
TUMBLING DOWN

indy and Angela were giddy with excitement about Mike's "Something is happening here" declaration. But I was still reserved. "I need to be responsible. If I get a signature from Chad by the fifteenth, I will rent the house if it is offered to me."

Mike had told me that he was a stickler for good credit, and he would not be able to offer the home to me if I had negative items on my report. I knew from my experience with the refinance that my credit was good, but I worried about the distant past coming back to bite me in the butt. Once again I saw this as a good way to put my future in God's hands.

I opened the email attachment my realtor sent and saw my new credit score on the very first page—785, an excellent score! And I was in good standing with every account for which I was solely responsible. But scanning to the bottom of the page, I saw the old negative accounts listed in a summary. They totaled eighteen. I took a deep breath and gave it to God, confident Mike would not hold my distant past against me if God was indeed moving on my behalf. We met at the rental home the following day, and I gave him everything he'd requested. He quickly perused the credit report and, thanks to the 785, asked me to write a deposit check, which he would only cash if my application was accepted by the owners. And then I'd have until the fifteenth of the month to decide.

It was October 1.

I was watering the plants on the front patio when I heard that still, small voice I had come to know and love. *Why are you still putting your hope in Chad?*

I shook it off. "I don't know what you are talking about, Lord. My hope is in you, not Chad. You know that." I moved the hose from the hibiscus to the hydrangea.

So why are you waiting for him to sign before you will grab hold of the double portion for your shame I have provided? Now I was beginning to feel uncomfortable. *I want you to take a step of faith.* Water dribbled out of the bottom of the hydrangea container as I reasoned with God. I needed to be responsible, didn't I? What if I couldn't get the signature from Chad and couldn't put the house on the market? What if he forced us back into court for any reason? I'd need money for that. As I made my way to a row of shrubs, I clearly heard the Lord. *You take this step of faith and secure the home I've provided, and I will get Chad's signature for you.*

I dropped the hose and stood still, focusing intently on the message. *I am your hope and your deliverer. You are where you are because of me. It will be to my glory to do this for you. I will not share my glory with Chad.*

It took a few days for me to grasp such a seemingly insane directive. I needed to know I was hearing God's voice and not being tricked by Satan. On October 3, I woke up early and shuffled to the kitchen table with my hot coffee. I began by singing a song of praise, as had become my custom. Then I fired up my iPad and read that day's devotional in *Streams in the Desert*, a wonderful book written in 1925 by L. B. Cowman.

His voice is a "gentle whisper." A whisper can hardly be heard, so it must be felt as a faint and steady pressure upon the heart and mind, like the touch of a morning breeze calmly moving across the soul. And when it is heeded, it quietly grows clearer in the inner ear of the heart. God's voice is directed to the ear of love, and true love is intent upon hearing even the faintest whisper.

Yet there comes a time when His love ceases to speak, when we do not respond to or believe his message. "God is love" (1 John 4:8), and if you want to know Him and His voice, you must continually listen to His gentle touches. So when you are about to say something in conversation with others, and you sense a gentle restraint from His quiet whisper, heed the restraint and refrain from speaking. And when you are about to pursue some course of action that seems perfectly clear and right, yet you sense in your spirit another path being suggested with the force of quiet conviction, heed that conviction. Follow the alternate course, even if the change of plans appears to be absolute folly from the perspective of human wisdom. Also learn to wait on God until he unfolds His will before you. Allow Him to develop all the plans of your heart and mind, and then let him accomplish them. Do not possess any wisdom of your own, for often His performance will appear to contradict the plan He gave you. God will seem to work against Himself, so simply listen, obey, and trust Him, even when it appears to be the greatest absurdity to do so. Ultimately, "we know that in all things God works for the good of those who love him" (Romans 8:28), but many times, in the initial stages of the performance of His plans: In His own world He is content to play a losing game. Therefore if you desire to know God's voice, never consider the final outcome or the possible results. Obey Him even when He asks you to move when you still see only darkness, for He Himself with be a glorious light within you. Then there will quickly spring up within your heart a knowledge of God and a fellowship with Him, which will be overpowering enough in themselves to hold you and Him together, even in the most severe tests and under the strongest pressures of life.[1]

I turned off the iPad and smiled. *I get it, Lord. And I will take this crazy leap.*

Later, while my friend and coworker Amber and I were together in the medication room, I filled her in on the latest twist. "So," I said, "I have decided that if Mike calls and tells me I have been approved for the home, I'm going to sign the lease." Right then, the left pocket of my scrubs vibrated. I had missed a phone call. Amber held her breath as I retrieved the voicemail message.

"Good morning, Jenny! It's Mike calling with the good news that you have been approved for the home. I want to know if I can deposit your check and reserve the home for you. Call me back." Amber and I jumped up and down a like silly girls. And I wasted no more time taking this step of faith.

Warrior Spirit

I wish I didn't have to report the nightmare that came next.

"Hurry! Open the car! Dad's gone insane! He choked me and threw me in the bushes!" Seth had texted me that he was in danger. When I arrived, he came tearing around the corner, running for his life.

And I wish I could report that when the police arrived, they believed our stories—Chad was a wife batterer, and now he was unleashing his violence on his kids.

But sadly, that's not how it went.

Seth had stood up to Chad, and things had taken a dark turn. Now my head was pounding and my heart was overwhelmed with heaviness. I peeked in on my son as he slept and the tears started to roll again. How long would evil be allowed to continue unchecked?

"Look honey," I said to Seth the next morning. "It's clear that our help is not coming from the police or the courts. Our help is in God. I'm glad you stood up to your dad. Maybe your actions will finally convince him to get the help he needs. Only time will tell. But we need to come up with a plan to keep you safe. What your dad did was not okay with God. And there is one thing I know for sure—you are going to see God move on your behalf. Mark my words."

My son got dressed and composed a text message for his dad. "Dear Dad, I love you very much and I always will. But when your anger takes over, it's like you're a different person. Your behavior is very intimidating and violent. I ran away because you were scaring me and I was afraid of you. When you tell me that I am a total disappointment and failure, it hurts me. And it's very confusing to have a dad tell you these things and then also tell you he loves you." Seth and I went to a favorite breakfast spot and tried to drown our sorrows in cinnamon rolls, eggs, and sausage.

Back home, I moped around the house and cried on and off. My son sat in his room staring at the computer. Both of us were completely traumatized by the assault, and a heaviness permeated the house. We went to dinner at Cindy's, but neither of us had the strength to be social or to hide our despair. The hopelessness in Seth's eyes was killing me. I knew that feeling too well.

During a prayer session in Michelle's garage that night, we interceded for Seth. Michelle spoke prayers of healing, safety, and blessing over him. Afterward, a woman named Beverly came up to me with fire in her eyes. "I don't want to be the weirdo that speaks up and says, 'I saw this and the Lord says that,' but I am telling you that your requests have been heard and answered. I mean, it is done. While we prayed, I saw God putting his sword back in his sheath. It's done-done."

I left the prayer meeting exhausted but at peace and came home to find my son sitting up in his room, texting friends, and laughing at YouTube videos. Looking totally renewed. The session had been a success. A few months prior, while on a surf trip with some friends, I'd been given the name "Warrior Spirit" by one of the local surfers because of my positivity and enthusiasm. As I got ready for bed, the Lord brought this memory to my attention. And then he brought to mind my experience at the previous Wednesday's church service. I'd gone forward for prayer and the beautiful woman who prayed over me specifically asked that I would gain a warrior spirit.

Okay, God. I want to live up to my name in this moment. Satan is hitting below the belt—coming after my kids. And I refuse to just lie down and take it. Give me the strength and courage of a warrior spirit, even in the face of such overwhelming darkness.

A couple days later, Cindy stopped by to check on me while I was carrying the first things into my new house. "I had a dream last night, Jen. There were three people in the dream. One of them for sure was Michael, and I don't know who the other two were. But I knew they were people who had passed on to heaven. Anyway, in the dream Michael was standing in front of you, and he had a message for you. I know this sounds weird, but he said, 'It's done. It's over. It's finished.' And then the dream ended."

I shook my head and smiled, thinking back to Beverly's vision. From an earthly perspective, things did not look very done. Things looked crazy undone. Unbelievably unfinished. Totally incomplete. But apparently, in the heavenly realm, the battle was finished, and I had won. I tucked this information away in my heart and got back to the business of unpacking boxes. I had things to put away in my new home. There was no time for despair or complaining. The time to shrink back was in the past.

Now was the time to press forward and live up to my new name. It was time to live as a Warrior Spirit.

24

JUST DON'T QUIT

I pulled the comforter up to my nose and giggled with delight. This was the softest, fluffiest bed I had ever owned. The dog nudged his way under the covers and curled his warm little body into my side. With the help of my friends, my muscular stepdad, and the body-builder types who helped him move all my worldly possessions in less than two hours, the transition into my new home had gone smoothly. I closed my eyes and was filled with peace and gratitude.

Within a couple of days, the moving boxes were empty and my kitchen cabinets and bathroom shelves were full. *Okay, God, I've stepped out in faith as I believe you directed me to. Now all I have to do is to sit back, relax, and watch you work.*

In Chad's mind, he was in the driver's seat. He had the power to bleed me dry over months and months.

After another grueling twelve-hour shift, I got in my car. I was toast, physically weary. Why was I suddenly unable to control my sobbing? I had endured far worse circumstances over the past two years than anything I was currently facing. I was so tired of Chad's taunts, his unchecked arrogance and boasting. After two years of battling and persevering, I was at the point of breaking. "How long do I have to do this, God?" I said out loud. "Why does he get to do whatever he wants, even physically assaulting our son with no consequences? Why aren't you standing up for me?"

As soon as the last question fell off of my lips, I felt alone and vulnerable. An intense darkness filled my car, and I was overwhelmed by a sense of despair. I heard a voice in my head whisper, "Why don't you just quit?"

I shook my head and tried to push the thought away.

"Just give up."

I gripped the steering wheel tightly and fought for breath. A heaviness pressed into my chest.

"It would have been better if you died."

The voice was right. I should have just died. I couldn't do this even one more second.

"You should end it now. Push the accelerator to the floor and get it over with."

And I did. I actually pushed the pedal to the floor and headed straight for an empty building. But within a couple of seconds, I regained my sanity. I took my foot off the accelerator. My car slowed. Was I was losing it? "Oh God, please help me. I can't do this anymore. I am so tired. So overwhelmed. Please, Jesus!"

It was a Thursday night, which meant Bible study at my house. Every single woman had texted to let me know they were not going to be able to make it—except one. I could barely stand from exhaustion, and I wanted to cancel. But after whatever that was that happened on the drive home, I knew that wasn't wise. My friend arrived, and I told her about my experience.

"I totally understand that level of despair," she said with compassion. Since there were only two of us, we decided to listen to one of the many sermons I had downloaded from my church. The message was perfectly timely, and the Spirit ministered to me and imparted hope and strength. I could go on. I could endure. As I closed in prayer, the power of the Spirit unexpectedly came over me. Right there in my living room, I had a throw-down with darkness.

"I will not quit!" I said boldly. "Do you hear me? Greater is he that is in me than he that is in this world, and you will not stop me! I will never give up! I will overcome because Jesus has overcome! He made a public spectacle out of you when he went to the Cross. His Spirit is living in me, and I mock you with my faith in Jesus. You will not stop me from telling other battered women that Jesus is real and he does what he says he came to do. I am going to break through your darkness with the light of God, and there is nothing you can do to stop me!" I opened my eyes. Had I freaked out my friend?

She was wide-eyed. "Did you see those things in your carpet?"

"What things?"

"I know this sounds crazy, but when you started praying, there were demonic-looking things right in front of you on the carpet."

"They aren't there anymore, are they?"

"No. They're gone." I told her I believed that what she saw was real. I could just imagine those little creeps, crouching down in my living room, licking their chops and waiting for a chance to pounce. But the resurrection power of Jesus wins, every time. I said goodbye to my friend and poured myself a glass of water. Suddenly my body was filled with heavenly goosebumps, and I lifted my hands to the sky. I burst out in songs of praises, and I could sense that my angels were singing with me and rooting for me. As if they were saying, " Hang in there. The Lord is good. You can do this."

I plopped my exhausted carcass into bed with a final word for my Lord. *If I wake up in the morning and the papers aren't there, I still trust you. It's okay. I know you have me.* In the morning I fired up my laptop just for the heck of it, and guess what I found? The real estate papers had been signed. All fifteen of them. I smiled as I got to signing and submitted the papers electronically.

A couple of hours later I received a text message from a neighbor letting me know that there was a for-sale sign in front of my house.

God keeps his promises, my friends.

Deliverance

Despite open houses with tons of traffic, multiple private realtor show-ings, and thousands of web views, we still had no offers. Chad wasn't signing the judgment, and my house wasn't selling. I had stepped into the Jordan River, but it didn't appear to be parting.

Instead of allowing lies and doubts to take root in my heart, I brought them to the Cross. I spent tearful hours lying face-down on the teal shag carpet of my new living room, petitioning God. Often I brought the same question. "How, Lord, are you going to stand up to Chad and deliver me from evil?" Finally, I received an answer while driving to work.

Okay, daughter, I keep giving you the answer through my Word, but you're just not getting it. So here it is plainly. I am the same yesterday, today, and forevermore. Because I had a purpose for my chosen people in days of old, I directed them take up arms and march into battles that were bigger than they. For my plans and my purposes, I forced them to face their enemies. And I will be the same with you. I have been pouring into you for two years. Week after week, I've seen to it my Word to you was restated from the pulpit, so that you would know you were hearing my voice. I've performed signs and wonders so that you would know my power. I have tested you and tried you, refined you, and built you up.

But if you are still waiting for a lightning bolt to come out of the sky and strike Chad, it isn't going to happen. The victories of life are not by might, nor by power, but by my Spirit. That doesn't mean you get to hide out, waiting for me to do my thing. You are going to stand up to your enemy, and I am going to be with you. You are my vessel. And you are my warrior. Your victory is at hand. Just don't quit.

I surveyed my circumstances, and they looked bad, crazy bad. Yet God had supernaturally restored my strength with a reassuring Word. So I surveyed something greater. I turned my eyes to watch the great I AM, who continued to row my wave-tossed boat with calm confidence. As my little vessel rose and fell with the surging waves, I looked toward the horizon. I would wholeheartedly embrace my God-given assignment:

Just don't quit.

25

THE FINAL STAND

*D*o *you really think it is a hard thing for me to sell your beauti-ful home by the beach?* This was the question the Spirit often posed during my prayer time. *Trust me. I'm working on the grand finale. It'll be for your good and my glory.* A grand finale sounded really good. Heck, I'd take any kind of finale. I frequently thought about Beverly's vision and Cindy's dream and was reminded that his ways were not my ways.

"I really want you to come to Cleansing Stream."[1] Michelle and the pod were planning to pile into an eight-passenger van and drive to a healing retreat. I really wanted to go, but the conference was on a Saturday and I was always scheduled to work on that day. I let her know I wouldn't be able to come along. But when I checked my schedule online, miraculously I wasn't down for Saturday. Woohoo! I jumped out of bed and danced in the shower. I knew God had made a way for me to attend, and I prepared myself to be blessed by whatever work he intended to do there.

It would take a completely separate book to adequately describe the revelation and healing that took place in my life at this one-day confer-ence. Suffice it to say that during this conference the Holy Spirit brought all the healing I had received over the past two years to a culmination. I received total clarity about why I had clung to lies about God and myself.

I finally understood why I had allowed myself to be abused for so long. And I came face to face with my spiritual opponents.

The spirit of fear. This spirit had been my mortal enemy for my entire life, and now, through the power of prayer and by cooperating with the Holy Spirit, I conquered this spirit for good.

The spirit of rejection. The door to this unclean spirit had been opened during my childhood. I had inadvertently adopted an "orphan heart" instead of a childlike heart. I made the decision to give God my orphan heart and adopt a childlike heart instead.

The religious spirit. The influence of this unclean spirit had led me to self-righteousness, pride, and legalism. It almost convinced me to allow myself to be killed, as if that were the more righteous path. I said a prayer and sent the religious spirit packing once and for all.

By the end of the day, I was emotionally exhausted—getting free is hard work—but also totally restored. The Cleansing Stream conference was the *piece de resistance* of God's transformative work in me. I knew this experience played a big part in my complete deliverance and would somehow be used in my grande finale.

Afterward, I felt prompted to write Chad a declaration. It was time for me to put on my battle gear, stand up to Chad, and declare my deliverance. No beating around the bush. No more tempering or manipulating things for the best response. No more shrinking back. After praying about it for a few days, the Lord woke me up at 3:30 a.m. one morning. *Enough stalling. Write it.* I put on my reading glasses, bowed my head, and asked the Holy Spirit to fill me as I wrote.

"The Final Stand"

You will recall that in an effort to settle things between us peacefully I paid my attorney to write the stipulated judgment. You wanted some changes, so once again I paid her to add those changes. You told me that once the changes were made that you would sign it "immediately.". . . When I sent you a text saying your actions would prove whether you were telling the truth, your response was even more hostile, and now I know why. It is because you were lying, just as you have lied over and over again for the last eighteen months. You lie, I believe you, and eighteen months later the divorce is still not finalized.

When I sent the requested changes to my attorney, I found out that the "simple edits" weren't simple after all. By removing your carefully selected sentences, you will regain access to the family home. I am paying the mortgage and the upkeep by myself, so I will be forced to pay for your housing. It is on the market and will hopefully sell at any moment, and you do not need access. . . . If either party wants to live in the home they must go to court and get an order before doing so. This protects both of us and ensures that the sale is not hindered in any way. You can sign either the original or the update—whichever you feel more comfortable with—but I am not going to allow you access while I am legally responsible for paying for everything myself. This would be folly. . . .

You are receiving everything the law states you are entitled to, even spousal support, which you should not be receiving because I was forced to flee from abuse. I tried to fight it in court and lost, and I have accepted this and continue to pay month after month without arguing. So again I will ask you, were you lying when you said you wanted to settle this out of court? I do not want to go back to court, but you need to know that I will do what it takes to finalize my divorce from you. I do not wish to simply divide assets, pay you support, and continue to be your wife. I am a human being with rights—one of which is to be divorced. Our marriage is over because of your behavior, not my choices as you so often say.

Year after year I pleaded with you to change your behavior. I prayed and I fasted. I begged God to heal you. So when your abuse continued, God became very small to me. I blamed him, certain he had forsaken me. When you threatened to maim and kill me,

I believed you. I was overwhelmed by the spirit of fear. Now that I am free from your threats and violence, I am no longer overwhelmed by the spirit of fear. In fact, I have authority over this spirit in the mighty name of Jesus. I am a daughter of the King, and nobody treats a daughter of the King that way.

When you were backing me into corners with your fists raised above me, my Daddy was there. When you tried to convince me to shoot myself in the head, my Daddy was there. When you nearly struck me with a baseball bat as I lay sobbing on our bed, my Daddy was there. When you terrorized me with reckless driving, my Daddy was there. When you threatened to "show me what a monster looks like" and I had to run and hide, my Daddy was there. When you threw things at me, my Daddy was there. When you mocked and screamed at me, my Daddy was there. My Daddy was there for everything, and when you hurt me, you hurt him.

What was happening to me all those years was vile sin in his eyes, a total affront to him. And yet you continue to walk in rebellion, claiming you have never done any of these things, when we both know the truth. Despite this, there is an amazing truth that comes from the redemption story: You are a pearl of great price to God. 1 John 1:9 says that if we confess our sins, he is faithful to forgive and to cleanse us from all unrighteousness. Even after everything you have done—all the violence, the rage, the lies—God will forgive and restore you, if you repent and turn from your wickedness.

Isaiah 44:20 says that "such a person feeds on ashes; a deluded heart misleads him; he cannot save himself, or say 'Is not this thing in my right hand a lie?'" This is referring to an idol, and in your case, your idol is you. Your reputation, your ego, your pride. This idolatry is leading you to flat out deny behaviors that at one time would have generated a tearful, heartfelt apology. I know you believe your own lies, but it is a delusion. And the spirit that is assuring you that you are the victim in all of this is not the Holy Spirit. I no longer believe that I have to stay in an abusive marriage and risk being killed or maimed in order to keep the law and stay in good graces with God. God's love and favor are mine because he is love, and it was never his will for me to be battered by you.

It is his will for you to humble yourself, confess your sin, admit what you have done, and ask for forgiveness. He wants to set you free . . . . All things are possible with God, but he never forces us to cooperate. . . . I am safe, I am delivered, I am healed, and I am free because of him. You believe that my future, my happiness, my finances are within your power, but you are wrong.

I plead with you to bow your knee to the authority of Jesus Christ. Turn from your rebellion and confess the truth to yourself and God so he can forgive and heal you. . . .

After walking by my computer several times in a two-hour period, I summoned the courage to push the send button. I felt a sense of triumph and peace and praised God for his transforming work in my life. But later that evening, I got a call from Barb letting me know that "Chad was very angry about something." I had a feeling my plea for repentance had fallen on deaf ears.

I was broke. I had no offers on the house. And I was likely going back to court.

Journal Entry:

Lord, I know you have a plan. You can turn all of this around in twenty-four hours. I trust your perfect timing, so I am just putting it out there . . . An offer on the home and a signature on the judgment would be the most unbelievable Christmas present ever.

That's the God I Serve

A few hours later, I was out running errands when my real estate agent called. "Well," he said, "we have an offer on the property. It's all cash and they've asked for a two-week escrow. They want to close by the December 23."

My heart starting racing. I lifted my hand to the sky. "Thank you, Jesus!"

"We need to go over the offer together—the three of us. Is that going to be a problem?" My freshly sent "Final Stand" declaration came to mind.

"No," I said. "I believe Chad will be on his best behavior."

That evening, I put some fettuccini and garlic bread on the table for my hungry boys and headed to the meeting. I arrived early and sat in my car and prayed. "Lord, my hope is in you."

Despite a few of Chad's typical power plays, I kept my cool. "Just give me a call when Chad makes a decision about the counter offer number," I said casually and sauntered out of the room. I drove to the double-portion-for-my-shame tract home in peace.

It was Tuesday, December 10.

By late Thursday evening, the counter offer was on its way. Friday morning I woke up early and opened the Bible to my current reading. I had made it all the way back around to Joshua again. "The LORD gave them rest on every side, just as he had sworn to their ancestors," I read. "Not one of their enemies withstood them; the LORD gave all their enemies into their hands. Not one of all the LORD's good promises to Israel failed; every one was fulfilled" (Joshua 21:44–45).

I dove headfirst into my busy workday. A couple of hours in, my pocket vibrated. I slipped into the utility room to read the text. "Well guys, congratulations. Your counter offer has been accepted and we're in escrow." I jumped up and down and squealed with delight. Christmas wish number one! My Heavenly Father knows how to give good gifts!

Thirty minutes later, my pocket vibrated again. When I exited the med room, I could feel my face beaming like Moses descending Mt.

Sinai, and I couldn't wait to spread the news to anyone who would listen. "Remember how, last week, I was out of money and I didn't have any offers on my home?" I blurted to my coworkers. "And how Chad wouldn't sign the judgment so I was headed back to court?"

"Yes . . ." came the curious replies.

"Well, I got a cash offer in the nick of time, and Chad signed the judgment. Boom, baby! That's the God I serve!"

And just like that, my fiery trial was over.

On December 13, 2013, after twenty-two years of living a secret life as a battered wife, and another two years rowing through a fierce storm, God gave me rest on every side. The spirit of fear, the religious spirit, the spirit of rejection—all of my enemies lay slain at my feet. All of my Lord's good promises were fulfilled.

Not only had I made it to the other side, I was forever changed because, through my trial, I had an up-close-and-personal encounter with the living, loving, almighty God who took the time to notice me, woo me, and rescue me. And the following was proved true in my life.

Every difficult task that comes across your path—every one that you would rather not do, that will take the most effort, cause the most pain, and be the greatest struggle—brings blessing with it. And refusing to do it regardless of the personal cost is to miss the blessing. Every difficult stretch of road on which you see the Master's footprints and along which he calls you to follow him leads unquestionably to blessings. And they are blessings you will never receive unless you travel the steep and thorny path. Every battlefield you encounter where you are required to draw your sword and fight the enemy, has the possibility of victory that will prove to be a rich blessing to your life. And every heavy burden you are called upon to lift hides within itself a miraculous secret of strength.[2]

26

YOU ARE THE MIRACLE

*I*n his great mercy, God had given me specific, but unexpected, answers to every one of my four big questions.

First, where the heck was my miracle?

Well, let's see. I'd spent the evening of May 13, 2012, huddled in a safe house for battered women—alone, terrified, and convinced of my powerlessness to stop my husband from eventually killing me. But by May 13, 2013, I was a woman composed, walking into a courtroom filled with the power of the Holy Spirit, ready to take the stand and face my abuser head-on. Ready to make my lifelong secret a matter of public record. Armed with Jesus, the truth, and nothing else.

God's answer to my question? *You are the miracle.*

I now believe God led me to court to test me, and I'd passed. I believe demonic forces were looking on, horrified, because God had readied me for what he was calling me to. I believe that the very same angels God dispatched to my side one year earlier were present, intently watching the scene unfold. And that, as I entered the courtroom and took my seat, a cry of victory could be heard in the heavens.

I'd also asked him, what about your promise that I would retrieve plunder from the fierce? It sure seemed like, most of the time, I was the one getting plundered.

You had your eye on the wrong plunder, dear one. God has answered, over time.

When I originally claimed the retrieve-plunder promise for myself, I'd been totally focused on material possessions. The real plunder was much more valuable.

Freedom.

Safety.

Healing.

Wholeness.

Spiritual deliverance.

Joy, peace, patience, kindness, goodness, faithfulness, gentleness, and self-control.

Nothing in this world compares to abiding in Jesus. Material plunder comes and goes, but the love of God endures forever. And his presence is priceless.

Often I have asked, where is my justice?

To which God answers, *I AM your justice.*

Once, while I was paddling out for a surf and talking things through with Jesus, I had asked him if Chad would ever pay for what he had done. When would justice finally be served? His reply was so soft and so sweet that it brought me to tears. *Every sin committed against you has already been paid for. I took it on myself when I went to the Cross. I died for all sin, even sin that is never confessed. I am your justice.* Wow. I walked along the shore and let that truth sink in.

I told you that your salvation was not going to come through the courts. I am your rescuer and your deliverer. Looking to this world for justice will only lead to disappointment. I now desire Jesus more than justice. And it's the cry of my heart. Why should I get a pass? Why should I be treated differently, when so many other women are denied justice by the courts of this world?

Yet I truly believe the cry of suffering women is reaching the ears of the Almighty, and his Spirit is rising up against the abuse of women. This is our time. His justice is only beginning to come into completion. I believe God is going to empower vulnerable women across the globe like never before, tear down the demonic strongholds keeping women bound in darkness, and perform miracles on their behalf. If God is for us, who can be against us?

But one other thing had me befuddled. "Lord," I prayed, "I thought my victory was going to come through my testimony."

It is, he replied.

I had to think about that for a while. Rereading my journal entry from my overnight stay in the safe house helped clarify. "That will be my message," I had written. "Jesus is real, and he does what he says he came to do." This was the only testimony that mattered.

Jesus *is* real, and he does what he says he came to do. I am a living, breathing testimony to the love, power, and mercy of Jesus. By the blood of the Lamb and the word of my testimony, I've overcome.

So can you.

AFTERWORD

Several years have passed since I completed my journey out of the darkness and finished the final chapter of this book. And I want to let you all know that choosing a life of freedom from abuse was the best decision I have ever made. When God asked me to follow him to freedom, he didn't let me know exactly what he had in store for me. He just made it clear that he didn't want me to die. He told me he would use my story to help others. He told me everything was going to be all right. I would like to tell you what "Everything is going to be all right" looks like.

Not long after my divorce was finalized, I began my single-woman-for-life, celibate, "Jesus is the only love of my life and the only one I will ever trust" crusade to end domestic violence around the globe. During a particularly powerful church service, I got knocked on my butt by the power of the Holy Spirit. I was worshipping with all of my heart when the Lord said, "I know I allowed you to experience extreme pain, but I healed you, right?" I responded with a heartfelt *Yes, Lord. You healed me.* Then he said, "If I can heal you from all of that pain and trauma, I can heal others too. I want you to preach my healing. Preach my healing."

At that moment, the pastor received a word for the congregation. "The Spirit says there are people here with unmet expectations. You prayed, you fasted, you did everything you could, but your marriage still ended in divorce. If this is you, I want you to come to the altar as we worship, and we will pray over you." I left my friends sitting in the pew and made my way to the front, tears streaming and hands stretched to heaven.

I heard the Lord ask, "Are we good?"

Yes, we are good, I responded in my heart. He asked again, and again I affirmed that we were good. *I am all yours. I'll do whatever you want. Go wherever you want. Say whatever you want me to say. I'm all in.*

Like me, you might think he then said something to the effect of "Now sell all of your possessions and spend your life leading other women to freedom," or "I am sending you to Africa." I had just promised full surrender, and there I stood at the altar, ready to respond in total obedience to his direction. But what he spoke next was completely unexpected.

"I have a husband for you. He's a good man. He's my man."

At this, my arms fell to my sides and I placed my hands on my hips. I opened my eyes, looked up, and said, "What?" I was so shocked. So stunned. So terrified. "No way. Never ever. I wasn't praying for that!" And yet I had just told him that we were good and had promised full surrender. I walked back to my seat feeling like I might throw up. My friends looked concerned, but when I told them what the Lord had said, those traitors were excited! Jumping up and down. Squealing like teen-aged girls at a boy-band concert. Hadn't they been listening when I so often declared that I was going to be single for the rest of my life?

When I got home, I had a heart to heart with God. Didn't he understand that I could never again love and trust someone enough to give them myself in marriage? Not after all I had been through. But I did have to admit that he had never hurt or lied to me. I felt him saying, "Trust me, Jen. I really want this for you." So finally I agreed to go through with his plan, but without any help on my part. There would be no dating. No eHarmony. God would have to bring him to me, because I sure wasn't going looking for a husband.

I started a new journal entry titled "Must Have Boaz Qualities." I made a list of non-negotiables. *No secret addictions. Not a liar. Not prone to anger. Must love God. Must be filled with the Spirit. Must be demonstrative in worship. Must have a heart for battered women and a willingness to support my ministry.* And then I listed something that wasn't spiritual, but that would make me happy. *Must love to dance.* I had always loved to dance. But during my marriage, if I dared to kick my heels at a wedding or some other event, my ex became angry and mocking, and accused me of trying to get attention. I'd always thought it would be nice to have someone to dance with.

At the same time, I was boldly proclaiming to the Lord and to my friends that my new marriage would be more of a business arrangement. We would serve the Lord together, and there wasn't going to be any of that doe-eyed, school-girl crush thing happening. I was too old for that silliness. By golly, I now operated with my head and not my heart!

On the very same night the Lord dropped the I-have-a-husband-for-you bomb on me, he told an exceptionally handsome man named Frank that, after twenty-five years out of state, it was time to return to California. Frank heard, "Sell everything and go now. The wife and family I promised you all those years ago is waiting for you." A few days later, Frank was in California. A few days after that, we met. God delivered my future husband to me through the most ridiculously intricate circumstances. And the moment Frank laid eyes on me, the Spirit told him, "That is your wife."

Despite my resistance, my fear, and several PTSD-initiated panic attacks, I slowly began to trust this honest and kind, hardworking and loving, Spirit-filled man of God. On our second date, while we hiked through the Angeles National Forest, I basically grilled Frank like a seasoned homicide detective. He took it like a man, answering all my questions with remarkable openness. All my marriage-as-a-business-arrangement talk flew right out the window. I couldn't eat. I couldn't sleep. I got butterflies whenever he called. I was just like a silly teenaged girl, and it was wonderful. The kicker? He loved to dance!

Frank first showed me his stuff at a friend's wedding. As the first slow song began, he led me by the hand to the dance floor. Holding me close, he sang the words of "I Can't Help Falling in Love with You" into my ear. We married a year later, under a Maui sunset on a white sand beach.

Today as we close in on five years of marriage, and as he remains the same man I met—caring, honest, and true—I'm finally experiencing the wedded bliss I'd only heard talked about. And it's safe to say that God over-delivered when he said everything was going to be all right. Not that my life and marriage are perfect. It all takes a lot of hard work. At times, one or both of us will respond out of our past wounds and hurt each other. But together we are growing and learning how to respond in the present. Most of the time, we laugh together when things are funny, cry together when things are sad, snuggle when it's cold, and hold each other tight when we close out the day in prayer.

I realize now that when God told me to preach his healing, he still had more healing in store. It is one thing to be healed as an individual. But it is quite another to be ready to love and trust someone again. The fact that I am now married to a good man is the part of my story that gives the abused women I meet the most hope. All of us want to be loved, and all of us deserve to be loved. And while I can't promise that every one of you will have an ending to your story like mine, I do know one thing. Everything will be all right.

In fact, everything will be more than all right. You can trust God to meet your needs and fulfill the desires of your heart because he loves you and has good plans for you. He does what he came to do.

Thank you for taking the time to read my happy ending. I can't wait to hear yours.

How to Recognize an Abusive Relationship

*W*henever I speak to a group of women, this is my message: Do not give yourself to someone who hurts you. It seems so simple as I write it now. It's not. It's confusing.

If you or I loved someone who was abusive all the time, it wouldn't be as confusing. Most of us know instinctively not to tolerate non-stop abuse. But that isn't how it typically goes. In between the cruelty, there are moments of kindness. Seemingly heartfelt professions of true love. Moving apologies. And the longer we stay in the relationship, the more confusing and complicated things become.

This is why, dear one, whether you've been with an abusive person for two weeks or twenty years, it is crucial that you face the truth, no matter how painful that may be. While each battered woman has her own unique story to tell—hopefully, a story of survival—common patterns emerge in most abusive relationships.

The Cycle of Abuse

Tension-Building Phase: The thoughtful, caring, and kind man you fell in love with becomes moody and distant. You sense something is bothering him, but he won't tell you what is wrong. He has shut down, and any effort you make in an attempt to open up a line of communication is rebuffed. You start to worry. You walk on eggshells and try to make your partner happy. You spend your day trying to figure out how to behave and what to say. You wonder what it is about you that is making him so upset. Fear and anxiety creep in.

Acting Out or Incident Phase: The tension builds to the boiling point, and your partner lashes out. He may scream at you or call you names and put you down. He may throw something at you or destroy something you cherish (perhaps a vase given to you by your grandmother or a framed photo of you and your best friend). He may physically or sexually assault you, leaving you numb and terrified. You may not even understand what "you did" to trigger the outburst, but your partner will make sure that by the end of the altercation you are certain that it is your fault. One of the hallmark signs of living with an abusive partner is that in his mind you will be the one in the wrong, and he will be the one in the right.

Reconciliation Phase: Once the incident of abuse has occurred, your partner may be afraid of experiencing negative consequences for his behavior, such as your leaving or telling someone. He will say he's sorry and promise not to repeat the behavior. He'll also minimize his actions and their effects on you. "I know it seemed like I was yelling at you, but I wasn't," he might say. "It's just that I love you so much and I was so upset. I didn't mean to grab your wrist so tightly. I never want to hurt you. You know how overly sensitive you can be." He will also make excuses for his behavior, which is a crafty way of switching the blame for his abuse to you. "You know how crazy jealous I get when you wear that dress. You really need to think about that before you leave this house. You aren't single anymore, remember that. I love you so much and I can't stand the thought of another man looking at *my* girl." Lacking knowledge about abuse makes you vulnerable to gullibility. This means you will likely believe what he says, accept his behavior as to some degree normal under the circumstances, and be willing to stay with him—even though deep down you know from past experience that he will repeat his abusive behavior eventually.

The Honeymoon or Calm Phase: The thoughtful, caring, and kind man you fell in love with has returned! He even bought you flowers and wrote the sweetest letter affirming his love for you. He does all the right things and knows how to make you happy. You are so relieved that you assure yourself things will be different from now on. While you are enjoying this period of calm, you may also be thinking about the last incident. It is hard to erase it from your mind. *Perhaps he was right about me,* you rationalize. You may accept his criticisms as truth and start to believe you actually deserved to be treated the way he treated you. You vow to love him and make the relationship the best it can be. Unfortunately, everything your partner is doing during this phase is a manipulation. Once he feels certain that he is again secure in the relationship, the power play will resume and the tension-building phase will start yet again.[1]

Certainly, I'd had bright red warning flags even while Chad and I were dating, incidents that provided much more insight into the man I was considering marrying than all the gifts and romantic nights out combined. Especially his "I'm such a loser—I couldn't even kill myself" confession. And then there was the time he raged at those guys at the local drive-thru for "looking at me." At the time, I was unable to recognize the danger signs.

Once we were married, Chad's behavior quickly began taking a toll on my physical and emotional well-being. At the time, I was unable to see the correlation between his behavior and my symptoms. Meanwhile, we were developing a toxic emotional bond during those reconciliation phases, as my batterer and I weathered horrific moments together.

I couldn't see that life was not handing us random, fateful moments of pain to deal with and move through together. Chad was *creating* those horrific moments with his mental instability and violence.

The following are some other common behaviors and tactics of abusers.

Secrecy and Isolation

One of the elements that must exist in order for abuse to continue is *secrecy*. Another is *isolation*. Neither are part of God's design for relationships.

It is important for an abuser to keep people away who might be willing to support his victim. He does this by focusing on negative things about the victim's family and friends, often being a "great listener" when she shares anything that is difficult about these relationships. He will pretend he cares, but he is actually leveraging these moments to reinforce the difficulties and cause strain in her relationships with others. He may also convince her that they need to spend time alone as a couple, assuring her that her relationship with him is the most important and should not be neglected. Another isolation tactic is intimidating her so she will say no to social engagements. It is common for him to reinforce the lie that he is the only person she can truly trust.

I know now that what was happening in my home was flat-out sin, and it could only exist in darkness. Had I stood up to the abuse early on, brought it out into the light, and trusted God instead of hiding in shame, perhaps things would have been different for me. But I was certain I had no one to turn to who would support my decision to leave. The truth was that any one of my friends, or even a neighbor, would have supported me if they knew what I was enduring. Only, nobody knew.

Jekyll and Hyde

One of the more confusing features for victims of abuse is how their abuser is often shrewd at transitioning between two polar-opposite personalities. Abusers have a remarkable ability to camouflage their dark side when in the public eye and may even appear as model citizens. This is called *compartmentalization*.

In simplified terms, [compartmentalization] enables a person to allow conflicting ideas to co-exist by keeping each of these different ideas in separate compartmentalized self-states, and doesn't allow them to interact.[2] This is how a baseball coach might be a loving father and husband while at the same time molesting a child on his team. It's how a pastor can deliver hellfire-and-brimstone sermons while having an affair. And it is how an abusive husband can also be a good friend, an excellent employee, and an all-around peaceful citizen. Explained from a spiritual standpoint, it's a crafty tool of Satan. At its root is a spirit of self-deception.

For the victim of domestic abuse, these kinds of conflicting behaviors in a partner contribute to the emotional confusion. The victim is likely to rationalize that they are indeed the cause of their partner's out-of-control behavior, just as he claims.

Minimization, Intimidation, and Control

The abuser has a number of other methods for making their victim unsure of herself. If she responds emotionally to her partner's outburst, she'll be accused of being overly sensitive. This is called *minimization*. After a while, not only will she accept his labels and verbal put-downs as truths, but she'll begin to question her own sanity—instead of her partner's. But please hear this: any woman living with a violent, unpredictable partner has good reason to respond with hysterics.

Other weapons in an abuser's arsenal are *intimidation* and *control*. Here's an example of how this plays out.

"What are you so upset about?" Chad asked with irritation while driving us home from a restaurant. I tried to stand up for myself. "I didn't like it when you grabbed my wrist so tightly. It hurt, and I don't like being manhandled."

Chad accelerated rapidly, swerved through traffic, and stopped so suddenly I hit my head against the windshield. "That hurt," I said, exiting the car.

"Oh, please. Stop being dramatic. You are such an actress." *Minimization.*

He slammed his car door so forcefully I jumped. Regret overwhelmed me. Why had I said "manhandled"? What was I thinking?

He shoved the front door open. "You know, I'm getting sick and tired of your crap. Do you really want to do this again?" Did I have a choice? It was already happening. "I can't believe you would accuse me of manhandling you! That is such crap, and I don't deserve it!" Wham! His fist hit the wall. *Intimidation.*

"Manhandled? Really, Jenny? I've never done anything but love you. And this is how you repay me? Everyone knows that you exaggerate." By the end of this interaction, I was in tears and wondering if maybe he was right about me. *Control.*

Spiritual Discernment

One of the important truths I tell others is, "It is not God's will for you to be abused." It *is*, on the other hand, very much Satan's will for you to be abused. In John 10:10 Jesus warns us that Satan is a thief who came to steal, kill, and destroy. He will do this by any and all available means, including using Scripture to keep us bound in abuse.

I knew the Scripture. "Love never fails." And I'd been earnest when I recited my wedding vows. Marriage to me was for keeps. So it wasn't a stretch for me to accept that God hated all divorce, and this is where taking Scripture out of context can get dangerous. Malachi 2:16 says, "'The man who hates and divorces his wife,' says the LORD, the God of Israel, 'does violence to the one he should protect,' says the LORD Almighty." This is clearly directed toward men in ancient Israel who were carelessly divorcing their wives with just a word—essentially sentencing them to starvation and death. This passage was meant to protect women from being cast aside, not keep them bound in abuse.

If only I'd known then what I know now—that Satan is a counterfeit and a liar. I bought his lies—hook, line, and sinker. I resigned myself to a life of secrecy, shame, and suffering, thinking this was my cross to bear.

The truth? What God abhors is evil and oppression. He never intended for his children to live and die in bondage. What the apostle Paul was communicating in 1 Corinthians was that God is love. It is only the love of God that *never* fails. His perfect love always hopes. His perfect love keeps no record of wrongs. This Bible passage had no relevance to my situation, though I failed to discern it.

If you are tormented, as was I, with questions about the spiritual implications of leaving an abusive marriage, I implore you to read the two books I have written that deal with this topic specifically. Each one can be read in thirty minutes from front to back and will bring freedom and truth. *Five Lies Every Battered Woman of Faith Needs to Stop Believing* addresses these questions from a biblical perspective. *What Not to Do If You Marry an Abuser: Lessons From the Girl Who Did Everything Wrong* delves into religious legalism and other important issues that keep women dangerously bound.

Hear this: God loves you whether or not you have been divorced.

Children

It's natural for someone on the outside to wonder why a woman who is being abused would bring a child into such a dangerous household. The answer is complicated. And let me assure you, I have endured countless hours of self-condemnation for subjecting my kids to my horrible situation.

I have a message for battered parents, something my counselor told me when I confessed the depth of my guilt and shame for bringing children into an abusive home. Here it is. God, and God alone, gives life. Your children and mine were destined to be. Their birthdays were written in the annals of time before the earth was formed.

I hereby release you from your guilt and shame, in the mighty name of Jesus.

Dear friend, I pray that you will take this information to heart and use it as a weapon against abuse. If you or your children are being physically harmed or sexually abused, you need to get out of the situation immediately. Put this book down, pack your things, and run. Run to a neighbor, a friend, a family member, or a coworker.

Franklin D. Roosevelt said, "Courage is not the absence of fear, but rather the assessment that something else is more important than fear." What could be more important than your very life and the life of your children? Don't wait another day for courage to come knocking at your door. Do it scared. Confide in someone. Create a plan of escape.

God is with you, and he will help you!

A Word to Pastors

You bear many burdens. The weight of this messy world must lay heavy on you whenever you close your eyes to pray. At times you probably look out over your congregation and wonder if anyone is really listening. We are listening. And because of the position God has given you, you wield the power either to hurt or to heal. To restore or to destroy. I ask that you remember this the next time a beat-down, worn-out, battered woman comes to you in search of answers.

Dare to question whether divorce is truly more an affront to God than a man's violence against the woman he vowed to love, honor, and cherish. Is divorce more grievous than a man emotionally isolating his wife while fulfilling perverted sexual fantasies in front of a computer screen? More grievous than a man sexually molesting his child? More grievous than his unrepentant addiction to drugs or alcohol, destroying wife and children by leaving their physical and emotional needs unmet?

I pray specifically that you will respond to the battered women in your flock—and there are many—with the courage and compassion of Christ. I beg you to take a stand against the evil of abuse against women and children in all its forms, even if other men in church leadership disrespect you for doing so. Let the church become a refuge for the battered woman and her kids. Give them food, for they hunger. Give them drink, for they thirst. Invite them in, for they are strangers. Look after them, for they are sick. Visit them, for they are in prison.

In doing so, you will speak healing into their weary souls, and the compassionate king you serve will call you blessed. May it lead to an inheritance for you in heaven.

NOTES

Foreword

1. National Coalition Against Domestic Violence, https://ncadv.org/statistics.
2. Blake Griffin Edwards, "Alarming Effects of Children's Exposure to Domestic Violence," *Psychology Today:* https://www.psychologytoday.com/us/blog/progress-notes/201902/alarming-effects-childrens-exposure-domestic-violence.
3. https://www.cdc.gov/violenceprevention/pdf/ipvbook-a.pdf.

Intro

1. Lambert, Carol A. "The Number of Women Murdered by a Partner Is Rising," *Psychology Today:* https://www.psychologytoday.com/us/blog/mind-games/201909/the-number-women-murdered-partner-is-rising (December 4, 2019).

Chapter 2

1. Katrina & the Waves, "Walking On Sunshine," track 1 on *Walking On Sunshine*, Attic-Capital, 1985, album.

Chapter 5

1. Todd A. Melf, "The Pulling Down of Strongholds," http://pastor-todd.tripod.com/id6.html (December 3, 2019).

Chapter 8

1. Lenore E. Walker, *The Battered Woman*, (New York: Harper and Row, 1987).

Chapter 9

1. Lundy Bancroft, *Why Does He Do That?: Inside the Minds of Angry and Controlling Men*, (Brantford, Ont.: W. Ross MacDonald School, Resource Services Library, 2008). Kindle version.

Chapter 10

1. Brian Doerksen, "I Lift My Eyes Up (Psalm 121)", track 9 on *Songs 4 Worship: Worship from the Heart of Ireland*, n.d., Integrity Hosanna Music, 2002, CD.

2. Alex Haley, *Roots: The Saga of an American Family*, (GB: Picador London, 1977).

Chapter 12

1. NEEDTOBREATHE, "Keep Your Eyes Open," track 10 on *The Reckoning*, Atlantic Records, 2011.

Chapter 13

1. For further study of demons and their influence on humans, see 2 Peter 2:4, Mark 7:25–26, Mark 9:17, Luke 4:33–34, Mark 5:2–5, Matthew 9:34.

Chapter 14

1. Bancroft, *Why Does He Do That?*

Chapter 16

1. Brennan Manning, *The Furious Longing of God*, (Colorado Springs, CO: David C. Cook Publishing, 2009).

Chapter 19

1. Manning, *Abba's Child: The Cry of the Heart for Intimate Belonging*, expanded ed. (Colorado Springs, CO: NavPress, 2015), 163.

Chapter 20

1. Ibid.

Chapter 23

1. L.B. Cowman, *Streams in the Desert*, updated ed. (Grand Rapids, MI: Zondervan, 1997), 471–472.

Chapter 25

1. The Cleansing Stream is an inner healing and deliverance ministry. Information about them can be found at www.cleansingstream. org.
2. Cowman, *Streams*, 242.

Appendix: How to Recognize an Abusive Relationship

1. Anastasia Belyh, "The Cycle of Abuse: Definition, Explained, Examples," https://www.cleverism.com/cycle-of-abuse/ (September 25, 2019).
2. Mark Leary and June Price-Tangney, *Handbook of Self and Identity*, 2d ed. (New York: Guillford Press, 2012), 58–61.

RECOMMENDED READING

Bancroft, Lundy. *Why Does He Do That? Inside the Minds of Angry and Controlling Men.*

Reading this book is a crucial first step. Shedding light on your partner's behavior, it will bring much-needed understanding to your situation.

Cleansing Stream Ministries. *Cleansing Stream Seminar Workbook.*

This workbook and retreat will bring dynamic change and healing as you learn to defeat the spiritual enemies in your life. Visit cleansingstream.org for more information.

Cowman, L. B. *Streams in the Desert.*

For anyone walking through the fiery furnace of abuse, this daily devotional is a must-have.

Faith, Jennifer. *Five Lies Every Battered Women of Faith Needs to Stop Believing.* This short but powerful book will help untangle tangled thinking and help lead you to the truth.

Faith, Jennifer. *What Not to Do If You Marry an Abuser: Lessons From the Girl Who Did Everything Wrong.* This is another quick read, packed with information that will equip you in your quest for freedom.

Manning, Brennan. *Abba's Child: The Cry of the Heart for Intimate Belonging.*

A book that will utterly transform false thinking about who God is and who you are. A key tool for breaking the strongholds that often plague battered women and restoring true identity.

White, Thomas B. *The Believer's Guide to Spiritual Warfare.*

With simple, effective tools and techniques, this book equips believers to take dominion over the dark forces bent on destroying them. The information is balanced and critical to deliverance.

Resources for Battered Women

National Domestic Violence Hotline:
www.thehotline.org
1-800-799-safe

Family Violence Prevention and Services Resource Centers:
http://www.acf.hhs.gov/programs/fysb/fv-centers
1-800-537-2238

Find a Shelter—Local Shelters and Domestic Violence Shelters:
http://shelters.welfareinfo.org

Healing and Hope. Words for Victims and Survivors of Domestic Violence, Abuse, and Trauma
http://lundybancroft.blogspot.com.au

**Please visit Jennifer's website for more resources,
inspiration, and hope.
www.jenniferfaith.org**